PEOPLE OVER POLITICS

Introduction

"Each time a man stands up for an ideal, or acts to improve the lot of others, or strikes out against injustice, he sends forth a tiny ripple of hope, and crossing each other from a million different centers of energy and daring, those ripples build a current that can sweep down the mightiest walls of oppression and resistance."- Robert F. Kennedy

The power of change often comes from the unlikeliest of people. From a child born in Bethlehem and raised in Nazareth, we have seen one of the great religious revolutions known in history. Nearly two thousand years later, we saw the strength in a tired seamstress who refused to leave her seat become the catalyst of the greatest civil rights movement in our history. And for a small town in southeast Georgia, this change came about in the historic election of its first African American Mayor in Jonathan McCollar.

In this memoir you will journey with Mayor McCollar as he tells his story of coming of age in the small town of Statesboro, GA and becoming its mayor. This riveting piece captures the struggles, heartaches, and lessons learned of a young man fighting for change in his city. It also sheds light on the fact that no community is exempt from the social and systemic issues that face America as a whole.

People Over Politics is the rallying cry for a movement that is focused on creating a true representative and transparent form of governing that places the interests of the people before political expediency. This message could not be any more pertinent than it is today in the heightened and politically charged environment that has consumed this nation. As millions of Americans struggle to navigate the new reality of Covid-19 and economic instability, now more than ever, it is time to put the People Over Politics.

CHAPTER ONE – MY ROOTS RUN DEEP

I believe that it is important for a person to understand their family's history and their heritage. I believe that when one understands this, it allows them to be better rooted in who they are and understand who they are not. I come from a family that has been rooted in Bulloch County, Georgia for a very long time. In the 1820 census you can find Alexander Mincey and Louisa Mincey who are the parents of Allen Mincey who is my great, great, grandfather. Public records show that Alex Mincey purchased the property that my mother currently lives on back in 1891. This particular transaction speaks volumes as to the kind of person he was as this time period is just 26 years removed from slavery. And for a Black man to acquire property in the deep south currently was not only a rare occurrence but a significant feat.

At the age of 47 these two men have meant much more to me and the person that I have become than I could have imagined at any other point in my life. Why? Well, they established the roots in the County that I call home and secondly Alex Mincey is the father of Estella Mincey McClouden, who is the woman that raised me since birth. For what it is worth, I have always considered Alex to be a lucky man as he was able to acquire some material things in his life during a very difficult time in American history and he had the fortune to be married to what legend tells as one of the most beautiful women in the region, Hester Summerlin.

Alex and his beautiful wife Hester had seven children. One of whom was Estella. She was born in 1910 and was married at a young age to Will McClouden. Her and Will had four children, but due to unfortunate circumstances one of them died while still an infant. The three remaining children, Herman, Elnita, and Virginia were the apples of their eyes. If there ever was a measuring stick for raising children during this time, I am sure Estella and Will would have been at the top of it.

Estella was small in stature and a spit fire. She believed in hard work and family. Every day she was up before sunrise feeding the chickens and working in the garden. Then for twenty years she would head off to the local college, Georgia Southern University, and fulfill her duties as a custodian. She believed that if you didn't work you were never going to have anything in life. But more than that, she instilled into me that if you really wanted to get ahead in life then you must help others.

The idea of helping people was something that she held onto deeply. I cannot tell you the number of people that came to stay with us when times get hard for them. I can remember a young cousin that came to stay with us when she had gotten pregnant. I watched closely as Estella would never utter a word that would pass any form of judgement or that would make her feel down about her situation. She welcomed her with open arms and the love that only she could provide. She would take care of her for the duration of the pregnancy and checked in on her after the first few months after the baby was born.

Estella was a special person. She was loyal to the end and it was God and family before everything else. I can recall being awakened in the middle of the night or early in the morning by a phone call from the local police department informing my grandmother that my uncle or one of my older cousins had been arrested for getting a little too rowdy at a club or some other form of trouble. My grandmother Virginia, Estella's daughter, would pitch a fit and Estella would not say a word for an hour or so. Then, sharp as a piece of iron, she would say, go get'em, while passing off a handful of money. Virginia would get in the car and kick rocks leaving the driveway pissed off on her way to go post bail. For Estella, it did not matter what you may have done. At the end of the day, you were family.

Though I could go through countless numbers of these stories that displayed the heart of Estella, and they all would be great, there is one instance that sticks firmly into my mind, and that is the story of Aunt Reatha. Aunt Reatha was one of the most beautifully spirited people I ever knew. She was fair skinned and had a distinctly raspy voice. Whenever she called, I could recognize her voice without even being on the phone. She worked as a housekeeper for some rich family in Chicago. My imagination used to run wild when I thought about how much money they must have had as I listened to the stories of the great adventures of this family.

Everyone knew that Aunt Reatha was without a doubt one of my favorite people. Whenever she was in town whatever I wanted was the task of the day. She visited us once or twice a year on her journey to Florida. One year she drove from Chicago with what looked like one of the biggest boats I had ever seen in my life in tow. On this trip she was hauling this boat to the Florida coast and stopped over for a few days to visit with us. I remember climbing into the boat and playing with the gears and buttons. I remember my grandmother Virginia yelling for me to get out of the boat and my Aunt Reatha telling her to leave me alone: "That boy's alright. Let him play." So, I continued to play and imagined what it would be like to be bouncing off the waves of the ocean as I zipped along in this powerful beast.

The visit with the boat stands out to me because this was the last time that I saw my Aunt Reatha healthy. Shortly after this visit she came down with a severe illness and the prognosis was not good. She eventually ended up moving in with us as she was too ill to take care of herself. I don't know how Estella did it, but she managed to do all her duties and take care of my Aunt. Every day she cooked three meals for her and the rest of the family while applying all sorts of ointments to ease the pain of my beloved Aunt. She would then go through the task of bathing her and making sure that she was able to find some sort of comfort.

Aunt Reatha did not live too much longer than a few weeks with us. As a young child observing all these things, I did not realize that what I was witnessing was the unconditional love that she had for her family. To Estella, it did not matter your condition or state; she loved you the same and was willing to make whatever sacrifices that were necessary to make you happy or to ease your pain. No matter how many times this process repeated, each time she gave her all and shed heartfelt tears as she laid to rest those that spent their last days with her.

Estella was never mistaken for being a rich woman, but what she lacked in wealth she made up for in her love for family. It was through the sacrifices that she made for her loved ones that you were able to see the spirit of the person that she really was. What she had was special. It was simply God given, because it takes a special kind of love and strength to be the anchor and healer of a family.

WILL

Tall, dark, lean, and full of pride were all personified in the mold of Will McClouden. He was a quiet man, but when he spoke, he meant business. He had a keen ability to read people. And once you had been read then he dealt with you accordingly. Everyone knew where they stood with him. Will also refused to work for any man but himself.

He kept his family fed by hunting and farming. His primary source of income was bootlegging. As legend has it, he and his partners had some of the best hooch in the region. People from miles around would come and get this "shine". His clientele ranged from ministers, to judges and politicians, to the people that ran the local juke joints and some of the "well respected" families that have their names engraved on our local streets and buildings on the campus of the local university. By the time I had been born he had stepped away from this life.

Will was the first man that I spent any considerable amount of time around, outside of my uncle Billy, in my formative years. I can remember thinking that he was one of the tallest people in the world. He was like a tall quiet giant that strolled through the house with his head nearly touching the ceiling, in my young eyes.

He was a very resourceful man that raised hogs and cooked food on an open fire in the yard. He would feed me squirrel, rabbit, and raccoon meat fresh from the flames of the open fire. He would also go into the garden and pick fresh collard greens and cook them in a kettle on an open flame. I am unsure of what he did to season those greens but my mouth waters just think-ing about them now. Though Will was a man of few words, he showed how much he cared by what he did for you. It was in these simple moments that his affection for me was captured.

If there was a story that ever captured the kind of man that Will was it has to be the one about him and his favorite hog. In his days of bootlegging all sorts of people would come by the house for short visits as they picked up their supply of the famous hooch. Well, as chance would have it, one of his favorite customers was a gentleman by the name of Mr. Hodges.

Mr. Hodges, as I am told, was an interesting character all unto himself, but he was a faithful customer. As the story goes, Will had a hog that seemed to be the envy of the area. The hog was a large male that came at the call of my great grandfather. This hog was also a little testy and would break out of the pin from time to time. As fate would have it Mr. Hodges saw the hog and offered to buy the hog, but Will refused to sell it to him. Visit after visit Mr. Hodges would offer to buy the hog and Will would decline.

After a while, it got downright uncomfortable for Mr. Hodges to come around because a great debate would ensue about selling the hog. In the last visit the debate turn into an argument that ended in a "nigga keep ya damn hog". As the days passed, Mr. Hodges, who lived down the road a bit, was not seen. So, as fate would have it, Will went to town for some supplies and upon his return his favorite hog was gone.

The hog being missing was not an unusual thing as he broke out of the pin all the time. However, in this case the pin was in the same condition as Will left it. He checked all the normal spots the hog would be, but he was not there. So, as he continued to check for the hog's whereabouts, he noticed that there were footprints and hoof prints around the pin. Being Will, he began to follow the tracks for a bit and soon realized that the tracks began to lead down the road towards Mr. Hodges house.

Will got so angry that if he could have gotten any blacker, he would have been mistaken for midnight itself. He rushed into the house, grabbed one of his shotguns and loaded it up. By this time Estella and the kids were home and they begged for him not to go but Will had made his mind up. He jumped into the wagon with his rifle and took off down the road towards Mr. Hodges house.

As Will pulled into Mr. Hodges yard he could see Mr. Hodges sitting on the porch drinking second rate hooch. Will pulled the wagon to a slow stop. Then Will said in his calm voice, "Hodges my hog seems to have gotten away. You haven't seen em have ya". Hodges raised up out of his seat and said, "Aint nobody saw ya damn hog and get on from round here ya damn nigga". Will replied, Hodges, I'm gone ask you again. Have you seen my hog?" Hodges, replied, I done told ya nigga I ain't seen no damn hog". Will then hollered, "SUEY!!! SUEY!!!". And low and behold the hog came bursting through Hodges fence sending every hog he had out into the neighboring fields and woods. The hog came right up to Will. Will then sent him off with a mighty Get! Hodges came running off the porch screaming, "Nigga ya gone fix my damn fence". Will calmly replies, "But you ain't got my damn hog, remember". And rode off back home on the trails of the hog.

Will was truly a man amongst men. He was fair, honest, and faithful to God and his family. Every fourth Sunday he sat in the deacon's corner at Antioch Missionary Baptist Church. When he died, there was an unfillable whole left in the family that we have yet to fill. From time to time, I sit and reflect on his life and what he meant to me. When my kids were younger, I would tell them some of the tall tales of Will with the hopes that they will pass them down to their children

HERMAN

Herman was Will and Estella's oldest child and a natural businessman. He, like many of the others of that time, had to resort to measures that were just outside of the law to make ends meet. Herman had the pride of his father and the work ethic of his mother. He refused to work for anyone else. So, like his father, he mastered the art of making moonshine and bootlegging liquor.

Herman worked these hustles until he was able to open his own restaurant called McClouden's Café. This small cafe slash juke joint was located on Grady Street Extension in Statesboro. There, he and his wife Emma Lee, sold some of the best BBQ, Soul Food and hamburgers in the area Monday through Friday. Then on the weekends it was the juke joint where everyone wanted to be. This little spot was in the middle of the black community and everyone was always there. The weekend nights seemed electric as the music waled from the jukebox and laughter filled the air.

Amid all this Herman was also the numbers man. For those of you who might not know, the numbers game is what predated the lottery system. Every night, except Sunday because you had to be somewhat respectful of Lord's day, the people could play the numbers.

The numbers game was hot! You picked a number between one and one hundred and entered to win the chance of making enough money to take care of the groceries for the week or the light bill for a month. If you were lucky, you could win enough money to open a small business or buy a new car. And at the center of all of this was my uncle Herman. He had two or three number houses across the city and the money poured in.

By the time he was 35 he owned several houses across the city and a farm that was more than one hundred acres. I was told that it was his vision for the farm to be turned into a Black owned golf course. This is a feat that would be impressive even for today's day and age, but even more so in the early 1960's.

When it came to making money, Herman was a man that would blur the line between what is right and wrong, but he was also someone that gave back to the people. Out of the land that was going to be a golf course, he donated five acres to a church so they could build a sanctuary for their members. He would have big celebrations where it seemed the whole town would come out to the farm and eat and fish until their hearts were content.

Tragically, at the age of 35 Herman dropped dead due to a massive heart attack. I often wondered what all he could have become if he had lived longer than those 35 years. I am sure I will never know, but one thing that I can attest to is that the business that he started went on to last another 25 years thanks to his wife Emma Lee and his children. What he started, became the means of how his family took care of themselves for at least one generation.

AUNT EMMA LEE

Emma Lee, the wife of Herman, was one of the sweetest people I have ever met. A beautiful brown skinned woman that understood the ideas of family and loyalty. Every morning she left her home, which was next door to the restaurant, and cooked her famous breakfast. It seemed that every hard-working black person in the city stopped by there for breakfast before heading in for a long day's work. The smell of bacon, sausages, eggs, and grits filled the neighborhood each morning as her doors swung back and forth with patrons coming and going.

After the busyness of the morning passed, she would prepare lunch and then set up shop in her little corner next to the window. In this spot she could see every person that came into the "store". She would sit there through lunch writing numbers for the people that dared to try their luck. She held on tightly to her numbers' receipts and the money bag as player after player came through the door placing their bets.

As a child, the numbers game was so exciting to me. I used to fantasize about what all we could buy if my grandmother hit the number big just one time. I pictured us moving into a fancy house, buying new clothes, and getting a fancy car. Suffice it to say, that it never happened, but there were some nights where my grandmother came home with a smile as big as the state of Georgia on her face because she had "hit" the number and a little relief had come to the family.

Though illegal, the numbers game was the life blood for many in the black community. Living in a largely segregated small southern town, the jobs for blacks in the city did not pay well. So, those in the black community had to "hustle" to make ends meet. The hustle of choice was the numbers game. This venture did not come without risk as a bad streak of luck could dig you deeper into a financial hole. However, for some people the risk was well worth the reward.

To make it simple, the numbers game was the gambling mechanism for the masses prior to the lottery system in Georgia. It was an industry that was dominated by the blacks in the city and when I say it "changed lives" it did, but if only for a little while. The smart winners were those that invested their earnings into opening a new business or doing something constructive for their families. Those that were not that smart spent their earnings on new cars and clothes. Nonetheless, most winners used their money to catch up on the bills they had accrued since the last time they won. This was smart considering this was during an era where credit was often based on who you knew and what family you came from.

Aunt Emma Lee, sweet, pretty, and hardworking was in the middle of all this excitement. Every day she worked hard to take care of the four small children that Herman left behind upon his death. Often, we hear the story of the poor widow, but this was not the case for Aunt Emma Lee. She was strong and resilient. She raised those kids without them ever missing a meal or not having clothes on their backs. As they grew, they began to work in the family business both legally and illegally.

This type of lifestyle, that I accepted as a norm, all ended in a flash with the sound of a telephone ring. Sitting in my living room with my grandmother the sound of the phone blared loudly as I watched TV and my grandmother played solitaire. She got up abruptly to go and answer the phone. I could not hear what was being said, but I vividly remember she and my great grandmother Estella going into one of the bedrooms and talking extremely low. They then left that room and went into the room with the money mattress. And all in a whisk my grandmother grabbed her purse and flew out the door and into her car. The Pontiac flew off down the road and my heart sank because it was evident that something bad had happened.

She returned a few hours later and not a word was spoken about the cause for the emergency. She returned to playing cards and my great grandmother Estella sat in her rocking chair as she normally would do at this time of day to watch the news and to catch up on her daily soap operas. Then, like a deer caught in headlights, I stared at the TV as the breaking news was that my dear Aunt Emma Lee had been busted for racketeering, or in layman terms "running numbers". If you believed the news, you would have thought that this sweet little lady was some type of a mob boss, but I could only see a woman who worked hard every day from sunup until sundown. She was at church each Sunday. She fed not only her children, but her children's children as well.

The irony with this story is that what is illegal and legal is all determined on the views of those that are in power. Shortly after my aunt's arrest, the state of Georgia legalized the lottery system. A system that is designed to fund public education and provide scholarships for students that can maintain a 3.0 GPA. It is also a system that is largely supported on the backs of the poor whose children, often, fail to meet the requirements to reap the benefits of a system in which their families fund.

PETE AND VIRGINIA

Virginia was the youngest of Will and Estella's children. I am going to go out on a limb and say she was the one that was truly spoiled rotten. I won't lay the blame entirely on Will and Estella as Herman and Elnita were just as much to blame. In her early years she was vibrant and full of life. She spent her days playing sports, going to parties, and living life to the fullest. Virginia was an overall good athlete, but the sport she loved was basketball.

While growing up, I could see the light in her eyes shine whenever she talked about playing basketball in her heyday. She bragged about how her team would travel from town to town "tearing up" the other teams they played. She often talked about how she would look into the crowd and see her brother Herman and her dad Will in the stands cheering her own. After high school, she went on to play basketball at Fort Valley State University, a Historically Black Institution that was in middle Georgia. I am not sure how long she played, but I can only assume that the time was short because she moved to Cleveland at a fairly young age and the stories of her days there were few.

When Virginia left Fort Valley she moved to Cleveland, Ohio to live with "Big Momma" and Uncle Tom. She moved there because she, like many other blacks during this time, believed that the north offered more opportunities than the segregated South. For blacks, the era of the great migration affected nearly every family that was based in the south. The railroads and bus lines were life passageways to freedom and opportunity as blacks were severely oppressed and disenfranchised from what we deemed today as simple freedoms.

Shortly after arriving in Cleveland she found a job and was off to a good start. She was beginning to live the life that she sat out to live in a new city bustling with new opportunities. Yet fate would take her for a spin as she would meet the man who would later become her husband and my grandfather. I am unsure as to how they met nor am I sure of the level of romanticism in their relationship, but a huge cloud of mystery looms over them.

During their marriage Virginia became addicted to alcohol, a condition that she would battle for the duration of her life. Their relationship was good, but there were those moments when it became volatile. Virginia had a reputation of being a firecracker at times when pushed and this situation was no different. My grandfather was a no-nonsense man in the truest form, but he did have his ways. However, I believe their relationship came to a clear understanding through a series of unfortunate events.

Virginia and my grandfather had a few arguments where he put his hands on her. Amid one of these arguments Virginia managed to get her hands on his gun. Pete, my grandfather, being no one's fool quickly realized that his life was in serious jeopardy and made a run for the door. Virginia was able to get off a shot or two, but that night God and speed was on Pete's side. They made amends and they both managed to keep their hands to themselves following that very disappointing chapter.

I was told by my mother that one of my earliest sentences or phrases as a child was "you drunk". When she told me this I was not surprised as one of my earliest memories was the fact my grandmother was fighting her addiction to alcohol. I can recall being in the car with her on one occasion and nearly running off the road and another where my uncle had to pull a man off of her in the parking lot of my Aunt's juke joint because she was too intoxicated to realize that the man was trying have sex with her.

These were all early memories. Memories that still haunt me today when I think about the horrors that addiction can play on a family. Amongst these memories are also the memories of her deciding that she was going to battle her addiction head on. It is in this space that I can remember going to AA meetings with her. I also remember the joy she had each time she was able to celebrate a year without alcohol. She had so much pride when she would return home with her chips for each year, she celebrated being alcohol free. She fought this fight for nearly 20 years.

When it comes to my grandfather Pete, there is so much mystery around him. I have been told so many different stories about him and the way that he made a living and the circumstances of his birth. In the middle of these stories there are a few things that I am certain of about him. The first is that he loved his family and took care of them extremely well and the second was that he adored his first-born grandson, me.

As a child my uncle would tell me stories of how the other kids in the neighborhood were not allowed to play with them because of my grandfather affiliation with some form of a mafia. How true this is I am unsure, but it raises a red flag for me when he can buy his son a new Cadillac and the son is two years away from being able to drive. Pete died before I turned a year old. Even now there are so many things that are left unanswered by his death. In an abrupt move he sent his family back down south. While the family was away, he supposedly fell asleep on the couch with a lit cigarette and it ignited a flame that eventually killed him and burned down his house. My uncle believes his father was killed well before the fire, but I guess we will never know the real answers revolving around his death.

Pete and Virginia had three kids, Billy, Sharon, and Patricia.

Growing up, my uncle Billy was one of the coolest dudes you could imagine. I can remember that on the weekends and the holidays it was like a show watching him get dressed to go to the club with the rest of our older cousins. I was born in 1974 and this was the heyday of his time. Billy stood about five feet eight inches tall and was a dark-skinned man. As a matter of fact, his nickname around town was Black and he believed himself to be a true lady's man. In fact, I can still hear granny's voice ringing through the house as she fussed about the phone ringing so much because of the girls that were calling him.

If you were to let my uncle tell the story, every young lady in the city wanted him or one of our cousins. And when it was time for them to all go out, he never let the ladies down. It seemed like it took hours for him to get dressed. It started with the touching up of the latest hair style he had. I would see the picture of Billy Dee Williams on hair product boxes or some other flashy black dude promising that not only would your hair look like theirs, but the women would love you as much as they loved them. I believe with those two promises you could have sold my uncle anything.

The next phase of the tradition was for him to take a hot bath and fill the house with the smells of the latest colognes. Then it was time to put on his fresh from the dry cleaners' clothes. My uncle was a huge fan of the Godfather and this showed in his attire. Every weekend, as he got dressed for the club, he would put on these very nice three-piece suits that were inspired by all the old gangsters and his idle Michael Corleone. To my young eyes these suits might as well have come fresh from the runways of some European fashion show. These suits were always freshly pressed from the cleaners and it seemed like he had so many of them along with all the trimmings to make him shine. He had the watches, chains, cufflinks, hats, belts and shoes. Each item glistened with from a fresh buffing with its specialty rag.

My uncle's shoe collection was second to none. He used to tell me that every man had to have a pair of Stacy Adams. I am not sure how true this was, but if there was a man in the world that did not have a pair of Stacy Adams then it was because my uncle had them stored away in his closet in a neatly ordered stack of boxes with the price tags still on them.

Before leaving he would parade around the house looking and smelling like a million dollars. His hair was flawless, and his shoes were shined to perfection. The suspenders fit perfectly, and the shirt was ironed with precision. His jewelry was noticeable, but not too flashy. The ties were in a perfect knot and his rings sparkled in the light. Last, but surely not least, a small, pearl handled .38 revolver went into the small of his back as he walked out the door believing that he was ready to conquer the world.

I used to lay in the bed while fantasizing about what it must have been like to be at the clubs that he frequented. I would imagine the people in the clubs dancing to some of the Motown legends or some Rick James. I could imagine them in the corners smoking on the little white joints and sipping on some type of liquor or some "expensive to us" wine. These images were easy for me because this is what I saw when I frequented my aunt's juke joint as a child. And so, to me, this had to be what the clubs were like.

During all this there was something truly special about my uncle. He was extremely intelligent and loved to read. He was also a great tennis player and his reputation to be able to hit a ball out of the park as a softball player preceded him. However, what made all this special was that he had been diagnosed with polio as a child and only had the use of one of his arms. For many, this would have been a barrier that would have stopped their progress, but for my uncle it was a non-factor.

Billy used to encourage me all the time to read as he was an avid reader. He would disappear for hours in the day into his room to read the latest novel, biography, or nonfiction piece. He read so much it was like living with a Harvard educated historian. His unique ability to discuss varying topics throughout history was amazing. He could discuss everything from Napoleon to the Civil Rights movement. He knew all the key actors and their personal stories. I believe that it was through him that I gained my love for history.

My uncle had a mind that if it had the right guidance, he could have been almost anything he wanted to be. He went to college at Savannah State University but ended up transferring back to my hometown to attend Georgia Southern University. He never finished at either institution, but he continued to be a lifelong learner. He would go off to different programs that we located across the state to learn a specific trade. At one time he went to become a welder. On another trip he went to become a CNA and still on another a business manager. After he would return from these programs, we would get a job and would seemingly do well for himself. Then like clockwork he would fall apart.

With all the attributes my uncle had his arch nemesis was substance abuse. He, like many others during this period, were the first casualties of the crack cocaine epidemic. During his era, it seemed like everyone drank and smoked a little weed, and every now and then they would do a line of cocaine. None of these things were perceived to be too major, because by Monday everything was back to normal and everyone was off to their jobs.

When crack was introduced to the city it was totally different. It was not like any other drug. It turned high school beauty queens into walking zombies and local high school heroes into the neighborhood junkie. Though this epidemic hit the entire nation like a storm, I would argue that it was nothing like the hell it brought into small towns across the country.

In the eighties we saw the politicalization of this epidemic via the "War on Drugs" and the "Just Say No" campaigns. It seemed that every politician wanted to run on being the toughest person on crime and being willing to pass the harshest penalties to keep our communities "safe". In hindsight we now see it was all a joke. The ills from these policies have had on families and vulnerable communities cannot be undone and are still hindering our nation today.

The neighborhoods that I played in as a child went from being the place where progressive blacks called home to being a shell of the promise that they used to possess. It seemed that the small businesses that once littered the black community all disappeared. Today, as I ride through my beloved neighborhoods, they are filled with dilapidated housing and the shells of where businesses used to be. It seems like it all happened in such a short period of time. As a kid, it seemed like there was a black owned business on every corner, but now it's not and the ones that are there are struggling to keep their doors open. Compared to the vibrant energy these neighborhoods had as a child, they look like ghost towns will proverbial tumbleweeds rolling through their streets.

My uncle? Well, he was no better than the rest of those poor souls that fell victim to this national pandemic. I can't say precisely when he became hooked on the drug, but what I can say is that he has not been the same since. He went from being a man that prided himself on looking good and enlightening his mind to being a shadow of his former self.

I firmly believe that if there was ever a family that was struck by the crack pandemic it was mine. It seemed like everywhere that I turned someone in my family was either selling the drug, using the drug, or going to prison because of the drug. My uncle was subject to two of the three, using and selling, but he failed miserably as he was unable to walk the fine line of being a dealer and an addict. I can't help but wonder what he might have become if this drug had never come into his life. I guess we will never know.

SHARON

Sharon was the middle child of Pete and Virginia. She was pretty, athletic, and smart. For the most part, she was the one that had the "it" factor. She had a personality that could light up any room. She, like her mom, was the life of the party. Sharon was truly a special person. She was a person that it seemed like every child that she ran into immediately fell in love with her. I guess you could say she was like the pied piper of the family as it related to the children. They would follow her wherever she would go, and I was no different.

When she graduated from high school she headed down to Tampa, Florida to attend the University of Tampa. She went on to graduate from the university and returned home to be one of the first African Americans to work "upstairs" at a local bank. When she got this job, everybody believed that she had made it. The entire family was so proud of her. I can still remember how pridefully the older folks in the family spoke of the great job she had down at First Bulloch Bank.

The salary from the new job brought about some financial freedom. As a result, she eventually moved out of the house with us and got her own place. It was a well decorated cinder block blue house that was right down the street from my aunt's juke joint. I was happy about this because whenever we went to "town" it was easy for me to run right down the street to see her.

I can still remember running through the front door of the house and searching until I found her. In life, if I knew nothing else, I knew that my aunt Sharon absolutely adored me, and it was straight joy whenever I found her. As time progressed, I noticed that the people that she normally hung around were beginning to disappear and new people were coming around. I knew the new faces, but they were new to my aunt's circle.

By this point in my life I knew that my aunt smoked weed, but that was no biggie to me as did half of my family and their friends. So, when I would walk in to see her smoking weed, I did not think too much about it. However, I began to see a change in her over time. She would go from this fun-loving person to a person that I could not recognize, mean and nasty.

It was not too long after this that she lost her job at the bank. At that time, it seemed like it was the worst thing in the world. I remember my grandmother storming through the house exclaiming how Sharon had lost that good job.

For a long time, I did not want to accept the fact that my aunt was on drugs. Of course, I heard all the whispering and sly remarks, but it was tough for me to imagine that a woman with so much joy, hope, and charm would throw her life away by using drugs. Coincidently, my mom, aunt and I were hanging out at my Aunt Emma Lee's café, and it was time for us to go. As usual it was my responsibility to round everyone up and get them into the car.

I had made my normal rounds and told my aunt Sharon that it was time to get ready to go. She said that was fine, but she had to take care of something right quick. So, me and my mom got into the car and waited for my aunt. As we waited, we started telling jokes and making each other laugh as we always do in our own corny little way. Time began to pass, and we realized that it was taking Sharon much longer than normal. So, my mom began to get somewhat pissed and told me to go find her.

I went into my aunt Emma Lee's house and saw my cousins sitting in the living room watching tv. Not seeing her there I figured that she was probably in the back of the house, so I cut through one of the bedrooms to head back that way. As I turned the corner, I saw my aunt smoking crack cocaine from a bent in soda can. My heart sank because what was an ugly rumor for me was now a known fact. Startled by seeing me there, she jerked as I turned away. I went back out to the car and as I was getting in my mom asked me where Sharon was. I told her she was in the house. Then she asked what she was doing, and I replied with a calm voice, "smoking rock". A few moments later Sharon came out of the house and got into the car. Before she could sit down, my mom looked at her and said, "Jonathan said that you were in their smoking rock.". Then with a straight face and with no hesitation my aunt replied, "awe Jonathan doesn't know what he is talking about.". It was at that moment that I knew that my aunt was gone.

As time progressed, we saw all the odd behavior traits that are associated with someone that has an addiction problem. She would leave home and be missing for days at a time. Her appearance began to change dramatically. This was a beautiful woman that was a presidential athlete with a personality that could brighten any room. However, as the addiction began to eat away at her, she only became a shell of what she was before. She had lost weight and her face began to sink in. When she was home, she would have dramatic mood swings where she would be happy one moment and looking for a means of escape the next.

Her addiction coupled with my uncle's addiction and my grandmother's recovery were at times very disruptive to our household. We would often receive that late-night call about my aunt getting into a fight with one of her boyfriends or my uncle being locked up. I can recall one night we received a call where she had gotten into a fight with one of her boyfriends. On this night, this one had struck her in the leg with a two by four so hard that it broke her leg instantly.

Ironically, if there were ever a walking definition of a functional crack addict, it was my aunt. As I mentioned early, she was a very smart woman. She was a woman that could do nearly anything that she wanted to if she put her mind to it. So, often she did.

My aunt devised what I recognize as being the most imaginative plan to be a full-time addict. She recognized that she was not going to be able to feed her addiction and manage a full-time job. So, she managed to get this temp job that worked her sparingly as a marketer for new products in grocery stores. Yes. She was the lady that would offer the samples of the latest meats or desserts in the store. She also recognized that there was no way that she could maintain a house and be an addict as well, so she moved back in with us. She kept up this ruse for several years until her body was too weak to deal with the pain of a broken heart. And tragically died from a massive heart attack after learning the night before that her best friend was killed at a local hotel by her boyfriend.

TRICIA

Tricia. This is a word that evokes so many different emotions for me. This is my mother. This is my friend. This is my sister. She has been everything that I needed when I needed it. Suffice it to say that I love my mother dearly and we have been on a journey together from the beginning.

One of the first stories I have ever heard about my mom dealt with her level of intelligence. As a young child growing up in Cleveland, Ohio she was performing at a gifted student's level in school and was recommended to go to a school for gifted children. Seemingly, this was exciting news because who wouldn't like for their child to have such a wonderful opportunity.

As a part of the acceptance process my grandparents had to go to the school for the in-take meeting. As they sat in the office the assigned administrator told them all about the wonderful resources the school had to offer and how the school would really be of great benefit for my mom. The conversation went on to include information about what an excellent opportunity this was for my mom. As the conversation continued, my grandfather asked the question, "what about Sharon and Billy?". The administrator tried to explain that this was an opportunity that was being offered to my mom as she has shown the ability to perform at a higher level than other students. My grandfather told the administrator that if all his kids can't come to the school then none of his kids would come to the school. So, they didn't, and she didn't. This is a moment in time that I often wonder about as I believe that my mom has the capacity to perform at any level intellectually. I also believe that it was this moment that would forever be a mark on her future.

My mom was like pretty much any other young black kid growing up in the 1970's. She wore her bell bottoms and stacks and listened to the latest music. I can recall seeing all the old photos of her at concerts or out at some small juke joint hanging out with her friends and family. I can only assume that it was during one of these moments that she met my father. Though I am unsure of how my mom and dad met, the one thing I do know is that it was totally under the wrong circumstances as she was only thirteen years old and he was in his twenties.

My mom gave birth to me when she was fourteen years old. I was the product of a young girl who had fallen for an older married man. The news of my mother's pregnancy rocked the family. However, true to form, the family stuck together. Besides, at that point, it was what it was because abortion was not an option. Disappointingly, this was not the case for our church. When word got out at church that one of its young members was pregnant. The church immediately kicked her out of the congregation.

I can't imagine what my mom was going through at that time mentally and emotionally. She was a young and unwedded mother-to-be. Regardless of the situation, she did not stop moving forward. She continued to go to school all the way up to the time of my birth and after she had me, she went straight back to school. Some of my earliest memories are of her getting up in the morning and catching the bus to go to school. The funny part behind these memories is that when I started school the same bus driver, Big Willie, was still driving our route.

After graduation she worked some odd jobs, but she ultimately ended up deciding to go off to college. She enrolled into a small junior college in Savannah, Georgia. While she was away in college, I would catch the Greyhound bus to Savannah to see her. Sitting at the front of the bus I eagerly waited for the bus to stop so I could rush off and jump into her arms. Being in my mother's arms as a little was the best feeling in the world to me.

As she went to school, she continued to work odd jobs to make money, but ultimately, she decided to come back to Statesboro. I can only imagine what she could have become if a few choices were different. In many ways I carry a form of guilt as I believe that if I had never been born her life could have turned out so much differently, but when I see how much my children adore her, I know that this was all a part of a great plan that we are all playing a small part in.

I have concluded that we spend a great portion of our adulthood attempting to quiet the demons of our childhood. Our insecurities and heartaches can largely be traced to events that happened to us as children. One of the deepest pains of my life was the desire to have that fairy tale relationship with my mother. However, in my early years a relationship was difficult to build. She was only 14 years old when she had me, so she was just a child herself. It is not until now that I can see that at that age, she was still emotionally immature and still needed to grow in many areas, but to a child the pain is still real.

CHAPTER II –
COMING OF AGE

Being a part of a Black family in rural southeast Georgia in the 1970's was serious. At that time the name of the game was survival. In our small town of Statesboro Blacks were not permitted to have businesses downtown in the decades prior to this. The closest we got to being downtown was a section of the city called Blue Front. Blue Front is where you wanted to be if you were Black and were a successful business owner. In this small section there were restaurants and all sorts of shops that were Black owned.

The one thing that I can say about the Black community in my city is that it always found a way to survive. For the businesses that were not able to locate to Blue Front they were usually operated out of the homes of the families that owned them or the family would build a makeshift building on their property and operate their businesses out of it.

The Westside of Statesboro is littered with the remnants of where businesses used to be. Still to this day, you can ride through this part of town and see where neighborhood candy stores, restaurants, and barbershops used to reside. Even as an adult, I can still recall how busy it seemed with all the businesses humming throughout the westside of the city. Growing up, I never had to leave this side of town to get anything that I needed. Breakfast was at Aunt Emma Lee's. I played video games and pool at Ebony Faces. A quick run to Rita Herald's or Jerry's stores for candy. For lunch, it was either a burger from Aunt Emma Lee's or a Chicken sandwich from Ebony Faces.

The Westside of the city had everything that you could ask for as a child. We played basketball at Blitch Street Park and in the summer that same park had a pool for everyone to enjoy. Being on this side of the city it just simply felt free and safe. We were able to roam the streets until the streetlights came on without any interruption.

I guess early memories for most people are always somewhat nostalgic in nature and as a parent these are the memories you want your children to have. For the most part, all these memories are good for me. However, during the summer following second grade a classmate of mine, Chris, and his brother lost their lives tragically in a drowning accident at the Blitch Street pool.

As I understand it, they snuck into the pool while it was closed and began to play. Unknown to them at the time, the drain in the pool had been turned on. During play, it is believed that one of the brothers had gotten stuck at the bottom of the pool because of the drain and the second brother tried to save him. Ultimately, they both lost their lives. The news of this tragic accident rocked our community and the lives of us that knew them and who were friends with them.

This was the first time that I had ever experienced the death of a peer. At that point in time it just seemed surreal. However, when we returned to school the following fall the young men were not there. It was at this point that the reality of their death really began to set in on us. Chris, I and the rest of our buddies were all supposed to be at Julia P Bryant Elementary having the most fun ever, but that was not the case and we would have to continue our life's journey without him.

My third-grade year in elementary school was a very significant year for me as far as my education was concerned. The year prior, the school system conducted some form of a standardized test. I have no idea as to what the name of this test was, but what I do know is that I did extremely well on it. In the days following the test several teachers congratulated me on how well

I did. Naturally, I was excited about the attention even if I had no idea as to what it meant. In hindsight, I did not understand the implications it was going to have on my future. I realize now that this was the year that launched the trajectory of my educational experience in the Bulloch County School System.

When I was in elementary school the tracking system was in place. For those that are unfamiliar with the tracking system, it was the way that students were separated amongst their peers based on their perceived educational ability. This was the education system's attempt to put students with like abilities in the same classes. Well, it turns out that this was just another means of segregating the students. In this tracking system, most of the White students tended to be in the upper tier of the classes. The Black students in these classes were either extremely smart or were a part of the Black upper class. Meaning their teachers were educators or had good jobs in the community. In the second tier of classes there were most of your Black kids with poorer White kids. In the third tier were all the remaining Black kids and any other poor minority. If there were any White kids in these courses, they tended to be extremely poor.

From third grade to fifth grade I saw my educational experience as being pretty much normal. I was your typical kid. I went to school for lunch, recess, and to hang out with my friends. The academic part was just the mustard I had to go through in order to get to the parts I liked. So, suffice it to say, that I was pretty much your average student, at best.

Academically, I never had any real problems in school until I got to sixth grade. For some reason, sixth grade was a tough year for me. There was no specific thing going on in my life that was much different than the years before. But for some reason, I just could not get it. I began to fall behind in my classes. Now, looking at this period in the rearview mirror, I recognize the significance of this period. For the first time in my life, I experienced what I believed to be classism amongst Blacks.

I can look back on this period and tell you that without a doubt my family was never mistaken for being rich. We, like many other families, had to load our clothes up in the car and go to the laundromat to wash our clothes. As we all know, the laundromat was not free. So, for a family that was counting all its nickels and dimes it was not cheap. My grandmother, with all her genius, decided to make me wear my clothes twice to school before putting them into the dirty clothes. Mind you, I had been doing this the entire time that I was in school and was never picked on by any of the kids.

Well, in sixth grade things took an unexpected turn. As for the first time, I ran into a teacher that simply did not like me. Now if you are wondering, the disdain was not because I was Black as she was Black. As a matter of fact, both of my teachers that year were Black women.

I noticed in her interactions with me that her tone was terse. I also noticed that whenever there was a group of us talking, she would only ask me to be quiet. One day her disdain for me became abundantly clear. The class was finishing up a fun activity, so it was a little loud during this transitionary period. As the class began to calm down, a high-pitched fart echoed through the room. Kids being kids, fell into a giggle fit. As I sat at my desk, quietly staring at a worksheet, the question was asked. Who did it? As the kids looked around the room, she angrily stared at me and said, "I know who did it. It is the same nasty joker that wears his clothes twice." The kids burst into a roaring laugh and I could hear them say, I know who she's talking about." If I could have disappeared in that moment I would have.

As the semester continued, I withdrew more and more from this teacher. Her tone towards me was unwavering. As a matter of fact, I can still remember the sick feeling that I used to get standing in the hallway when we were changing to her classroom. At some point, I got used to the treatment and began to relax a little in her class. Being an average sixth grader, a friend and I were talking, and she heard us. To say she got upset would be a clear understatement. In her enraged mode she called me into the hallway swinging her paddle around. I got up and walked towards the door realizing that I never heard the name of the person that I was talking to called. As she came into the hallway she began to fuss and poke me in the shoulder. I am unsure what she was saying, but the one thing I was sure of was that this entire situation felt wrong. She then told me to "assume the position". As I placed my hands on the wall, I recall her swinging with all her might and striking me with the paddle. Before she could fire off the next two licks I stood up and looked at her in her eyes and said to her, "That is enough." and walked back into the classroom. This was the first time that my inner conviction had allowed me to stand up for what was right against a perceived authority figure that had clearly gone too far. For the duration of that school year, she and I did not speak a word to each other.

This was a significant point for me in my life. I finally understood what I had been told all my life: no one can do no more to you than what you allow them to do. This was a saying that my great grandmother used to tell me all the time. Refusing to ever be considered a victim again and being picked on for wearing my clothes twice, I got my first job.

At the time the local newspaper ran a free Rent-A-Kid ad section in the classifieds of the newspaper. It was for kids that were willing to do little odd jobs for pay. I submitted my information and it was not too long before my phone rang with a great opportunity. The voice on the other end of the line was that of an elderly white gentleman that needed some yard work done at his home. He lived in the Woodlawn neighborhood, which was and still is, a very distinguished area of the city with lots of history.

Early on that following Monday morning my grandmother took me to his home and dropped me off. I remember walking up to the front door and ringing the doorbell and thinking to myself that I wanted to live in a neighborhood like this one day. The gentleman came to the door and invited me into his home. We went into the kitchen where he had a little table that sat next to a large window. He offered me breakfast, but I kindly declined, and we began to discuss the jobs he had for me. The list was long, but doable over the course of the summer.

In the beginning I would arrive around 8:00 am with the gentleman greeting me at the kitchen door. I would eat a little breakfast with him in the morning and have a little conversation before I would head out and start the tasks for the day. I would cut the grass on a regular schedule and rake the clippings when I was done. I also did work in the rose bed and other odd jobs around the house. As time progressed, I came to realize that the time that I spent there was not so much about the work I was doing but the work he was doing with me.

It was at the breakfast table that he talked with me about all sorts of things. We talked about everything from the news, to sports, and about people in general. Looking back, I believe the gentleman had become somewhat attached to me, and I him. During the time I spent with him there he taught me a lot of simple things, but the one thing that he taught me that has stuck with me the most is the management of a checkbook. He taught me how to sign a check and to be sure to put everything in the ledger. Until this day whenever I sign a check, I think about him. After that summer I never saw him again, but I have thought of him often.

When that summer ended, I had met my goals of working to save enough money to help buy school clothes for the upcoming fall. Next to Christmas, the best day of the year is the first day of school and it has nothing to do with academics. There was nothing like coming to school on the first day "fresh to death" in your new gear. If there was a close runner up to this day, it would be the day you go shopping to get your clothes. And this year was going to be the best year ever. Why? Because we were going to Allied!!!

Allied was a small store located in the neighboring town of Metter. It was known to have the best discounts. This year Allied was in for a treat because I had some money that was burning a hole in my pocket. I can't remember how much money I was able to save over the course of that summer, but it was more than I had ever had. So, when we left the store it felt like I was on the Lifestyles of the Rich and Famous. I chuckle as I write this as I only had a few pairs of no name jeans, a couple of no name shirts, and a pair of no name shoes. However, the thrill for me was that I was able to spend my own money and do for myself.

Middle school is where I began to find my identity and develop my own voice. By this time, I was spending more time with friends than family. I don't see this part of my life being too much different than any other kid's life at this point. However, what I can say is that I really enjoyed my middle school experience much more than that of my sixth-grade year. It seemed like every teacher I had over the course of those two years had a genuine interest in me and my education.

My seventh-grade year is the year that I was first introduced to the world of politics. I decided to run for vice president of my class. I had never run for any office before and had never shown any interest in doing so. I am still unsure as to why I did it, but it was clear that the support system, both at home and school, the other candidates had was much different than mine. During the week of the election, the entire school was littered with signs and candidates passed out candy in the hall. When the elections ended, I was nowhere in the running. At the time, this was not an experience that swayed my one way or another, but in reflection it is clear to see the role that socioeconomics play in the development and life experiences of a young person.

The summer after my eighth-grade year was exciting. I didn't go anywhere specific, but I had the opportunity to learn my city in ways that I never knew. I hung out with friends until late into the night. In between telling jokes and eating an unhealthy amount of McDonald's we spent our time "rapping" to the girls. Keep in mind that this was prior to social media, texting, and the sort. So, you had to really have a little swag if you were going to get any play. I believe this summer was so special because this is a time where I can specifically identify a loss of innocence.

I entered ninth grade full of excitement. I was going to the "big" high school, Statesboro High. The summer prior I had heard all the freshmen horror stories. I heard the stories of how freshmen were thrown in the trash cans by the upperclassmen or beat up in the bathrooms. Until this day, I don't know if any of these stories were ever true, but when I got to high school it seemed as though I was either related to or a friend of everyone that was there. And those that I was not related to were all pretty cool.

Prior to going to high school, friends of my neighbors were professors at Georgia Southern University which is in my hometown. I would hear the young professors' talk about college life and discuss all the hottest topics of the day. It was through them that I began to her the names of Black historical figures who transformed our country. I was so inspired by their conversations that I made up my mind that I wanted to go off to college when I graduated from high school.

Just before the first day of school my freshman year, me and a few friends caught a ride out to the high school to sign up for college prep classes. As we pulled up to the school, we were overjoyed that in a few days we were going to be "big time" high school students. As we rushed into the school and into the counselors' office, I could feel my heart pounding because I knew that this was a big step for me.

I sat down with the counselor and told her that I wanted to attend college and needed to be placed into college prep courses. The counselor asked a few questions about my ability to do the work and I assured her that I could and would do the work. Besides, I had been watching the Cosby Show and A Different World, so I knew I was ready. Plus, they made everything seem so easy about college.

The first semester of my freshman year was the best and worst experience you could possibly imagine. Socially, it was clicking on all cylinders for me. Academically, it was like being in a war-zone. It was simply awful.

On the first day of walking into the college prep courses, I immediately knew that I was no longer in Kansas. The demographic make of the classes were totally different from those that I had been in previously. The kids in these classes clearly did not come from the same neighborhoods as the kids that I was accustomed to being in class with and they surely did not look like them. For the most part the students were White and well off by Statesboro standards. There were a few Black students in the classes, but they came from middle classes families with both mom and dad in the household.

I felt like I stuck out like a sore thumb every day that I walked into these classes. On the first day it was a demographic thing. The rest of the days it became clear by the way I dressed and spoke that I did not fit in. I remember feeling alone as I didn't fit in with the White students nor did I fit in with the Black students. And to top it off, the work was like something I never saw before.

Leaping from general classes to college prep was no joking matter. In the general classes, I didn't have to study. All I had to do was listen in class and give the work a quick once over right before the test and I was good. As a result, I never developed the study habits that were needed for these types of courses. By the end of the semester, I could not tell if I was in a math class or an English class. And to make matters worse, I didn't feel like I could make a connection with any of the teachers.

Going to these classes became a spiritual burden to me. I would come into the class right before the bell would ring and just sit in my desk and not participate. Some days I would pretend to be asleep so that the teacher would not call on me. I felt so out of place. I began to believe that I was not smart enough or worthy enough to be in those courses.

I often say that no one is going to be tougher on me than me. Well, there is an exception to the rule, my mom. If things were not bad enough as is, the universe conspired against me and scheduled a parent-teacher conference. This perhaps was one of the worst moments in my life.

It seemed that the day of the parent teacher conference moved slower than any other day in history. The anxiety of my mom meeting with my homeroom teacher to discuss my grades was too much to bear. I knew I had not been performing well, but it still did not register how severe of a situation this was.

At the end of the school day, I got on the bus to head home. My mom was working at Willingway hospital in the kitchen and did not get off until eleven o'clock. Since I was a baby, I have always lived with my great-grandmother and grandmother along with my mom, but when I was in elementary school my mother moved out to go to college in Savannah while I stayed behind. When she returned to Statesboro, she got a place of her own and I continued to stay with my grandmother and great-grandmother. Because of this she would visit daily and call in the evening to check-in prior to her going to bed. Well, on this night I heard her car pulling into the yard after a long day of work.

As I laid in the bed, I could hear the front door swing open. I heard her calm voice speaking to my grandmother and great-grandmother. It was this tone that let me know that I was in for. It was surely the calm before the storm. Then, like the giant in the sky, I could hear her footsteps through the house as she made her way back to my room.

She flew into my room and I laid there thinking to myself that there was no way that I was going to survive this as she snatched the cord to turn on the light. She began to yell, but the sound of yelling quickly turned to the sounds of her sobbing. She began to sob uncontrollably. With tears rolling down her cheeks she told me that my teacher had advised her that I would not be graduating from high school and if I did it would not be with my class. As I stood there in that moment, my heart sank as I realized that the pain that mother felt was because of me. It was in that instance that I vowed that I would never be the reason she would ever shed a tear again.

As the semester went on all my hurt and self-doubt built up inside of me until the point, I finally decided to go to the counselor's office to withdraw from the college prep courses and return to the general track. When I walked through the doors of the counselor's office all I can remember is feeling defeated. This was the first time in my life that I felt like there was nothing I could do. I sat in the chair feeling nothing but darkness consuming me. Then, I heard my name called.

Ms. Collier was everyone's favorite counselor. I am not sure how old she was, but she was a very beautiful woman with some slight gray in her hair. She was a confident but soft-spoken woman. She very calmly sat me down and asked how she could help me. I said in a very shaky voice that I needed to withdraw from the college prep courses and return to the general track. She looked over my grades and asked me what I thought the problem was and I responded by telling her that it was me. I was the problem. I simply felt that I could not do the work. Then I broke down into an inconsolable cry as all the emotions associated with self-doubt and guilt were released. As I cried, she spoke calming and reassuring words to me while letting me know that all was not lost.

The next semester I returned to the general classes. They were filled with all the familiar faces that I loved and the friends that I knew. Over the course of the semester I worked to bring my averages up, but it was not enough. By the end of the semester, I was only able to earn three and half credits out of a possible six. So, you guessed it, I was back in a ninth-grade homeroom again the following year.

Typically, I looked forward to the summers as they were filled with lazy days and having big fun with my friends. However, the summer following my freshman year was different. From day one I was filled with anxiety about the first day of the new school year. And if the anxiety was not enough, going to the mailbox the week following the last day of class and getting my report card to see that I was officially "retained" added to the darkness of the moment.

There are those moments in our lives that we just simply can't get over no matter how long ago they were. And for me, that day I went to the mailbox and saw that I had received my report card was one of those days. Up until this point I had always heard about people being left back. Heck, I even knew people that had been left back, but it was never me. Well, this time it was. My heart sank and my body became numb as I stood next to the road and just gazed at my report card with a nine scribed into the place where it said next year's grade assignment. For the first time, I had come face to face with failure.

As the summer progressed, the thought of being left back always rang in the back of my mind. My friends and I would be out having what would seem to be the best time ever, and then in the back of my mind I would hear a voice say, "You know you got left back, right". The thought of having to go back to school and face the embarrassment of being in the same grade as the previous year was inescapable. It seemed that every day that passed the dread of the first day of school grew stronger.

In years passed the days leading up to the first day of school were filled with the excitement of getting new clothes and seeing the friends you had not seen the entire summer. This year was not like that at all. I could have cared less about the new clothes and the last thing that I wanted was for my friends to see me. Especially, if they were watching me walk down to the ninth-grade wing of the school.

Inevitably, the first day of school came and it was as dark as I thought it would be. It seemed that the entire morning was moving in slow motion. I got out of bed and just sat there for a while. I washed up and got dressed. I grabbed a bite to eat and as I walked out the door, I heard Granny say to me, "Now, you get yo lesson this year". I jumped on the bus and the loud chatter was all background noise the entire way to school. When we arrived at the exchange school to get on the bus that was taking us to the high school my conversation was little to none and I was even quieter on the ride to the school.

The bus pulled up to the school and it seemed like the breezeway was the longest it had ever been as we made our way to the main hall. Main hall was the spot where all the students hung out until it was time for us to go to our homerooms. You could hear the chatter from all the students. The girls were giving the guys hugs and laughter was everywhere. I tried my best to participate, but what I knew was that I was about to be the center of attention as the people saw me walking down to the ninth-grade wing.

As the bell rang to let us know to head to our homerooms, I hung around in the main hall until it was nearly empty. Then I decided that I would head down to "THE WING". As I was walking towards my homeroom, I noticed a few familiar faces. It seemed that I was not the only person that fell victim to the freshman bug. I am not going to say that I was happy to see that others were making the same walk as I, but it did ease my load to know that I was not alone.

In my second year of high school I was in an "I don't care" state of mind. I felt detached. I was still hanging out with friends and had grown numb to the fact that I was repeating a grade. Academically, I did enough to pass, but anything beyond that I was not having it. My good friend Big J, who always was my neighbor, had acclimated extremely well and was back to being his normal self.

Big J and I were like two peas in a pod and had been like that since fifth grade. If you saw him then you saw me. During this time, we would go over to Tandy and Jennifer's house and hang out with them and their aunt and uncle. They had just moved down to the Boro from North Carolina. They moved to the area because their uncle was stationed here with the Army as a local recruiter.

The girls were new to the area so as they met people, they would ask what we thought of them or whether we hung out with them. Well, at this point in our lives we hung out with a very small group of people daily, but coming from a small town, we knew everybody. In conversation one day they asked us about a group of guys that called themselves Gentlemen Guess Club. They wanted to know if we hung out with them and the sort. If you were from the Boro, you knew about Gentlemen's Guess Club. So, when they asked, we were like yes, we know them and they are cool, but we didn't hang out with them.

Jennifer and Tandy had a little cousin, Kenya, that was in elementary school at the time and she was crazy about me and Big J. She would just light up every time we came over to hang out with the girls. Unknown to us, one of the guys in Gentle Guest Club had a crush on one of the sisters. Until this day, I don't know who the guy was, but whoever it was, their little cousin did not care for them. As I understand it something transpired that upset Kenya and she told the guy that we said that we did not mess with them not understanding that we were simply saying we didn't hang out with them.

By this time, things were picking up for me at school and I was getting back to my old self socially. So, me and Big J were hanging out on the wall in the second hall laughing and joking excited about it being homecoming week. Then out of the blue we were surrounded by members of Gentlemen's Guest Club. It had to be seven or eight of them. And the only thing that I could hear the spokesman for the group say was that we heard that y'all were talking about us. Big J and I were confused as hell, because these were people that we thought were cool with even though we didn't hang out with them. So, Big J, in Big J fashion, started asking them what you are talking about? Meanwhile, the spokesman continued to repeat, I heard y'all been talking about us? By this time it had become evident that these guys were not here out of rationality and the only thing I could hear in my head was the advice of the Big J's old brother saying, "If you are going to get jumped, you punch the biggest one in the face first".

As my eyes searched through the group, I saw the guy that I was going to hit in the face first. I slowly slid to his blind spot and patiently began to wait for the right moment. I was quiet and no longer engaging in the conversation. Then out of the blue, it seemed like the whole basketball team came from nowhere and broke through the crowd. Whew!!!! We were rescued!!! Mitch, Crecy, Keith, Dregg, and the crew saved the day. For the first time, it was good that Big J was a baller and I had a lot of family. Crecy just busted up in the middle of everything and had only one question. "What da bit'ness is?!?!?"

To this point, Big J and I still had no idea what was going. We walked away confused and in disbelief. We went to our home-rooms and throughout the rest of the day with no problems. However, this became a big problem for other people. The en-tire week of homecoming was filled with talk. Then on home-coming day it reached its peak.

The incident that occurred with us on Monday had somehow turned into an excuse for some people that had some issues to kick up a little dust throughout the week. In the process, we found out that we came into play because of what an elemen-tary kid had said, and her older cousin Jennifer played it up more than what it should have been. So, the day prior to home-coming Big J's cousin Broonie caught wind of what was happen-ing. Broonie, and what seemed like the enter school, rampaged through the halls searching for Jennifer, but she was nowhere to be found. I never told anyone this but, I was relieved that she was not found because Broonie was nothing to play with and her fight game was something serious. It is scary to even im-agine how that could have turned out.

The next morning was homecoming day however, for some people it was going to be a day of reckoning. When we arrived into the main hall that morning it seemed like the entire school was on one wall and a few of the guys from Gentlemen's Guest Club were on the other. Mind you, that no one ever stood on the wall across from them until this morning. The chatter was loud, and the atmosphere was crazy. I remember seeing Stevie walking around with a book in his hand saying that he was ready to get this thing start and was ready to slap one of those "niggas" in the face with a book. Tyrone came up to me and pulled me to the back of the crowd. As he pulled this glove with a large thick piece of metal in its center, he said to me, "Jay put this on. You too little. If you get in the middle of this thang, bust one of them niggas in the head with this. Don't make a fist because it's going to break your hand".

So, there we were in the middle of the main hall. The crowd was pulsating, and the spectators were egging the crowd on. Then a voice yelled out." Big J what we gone do?!" And in a very nonchalant why he said, "Man I ain't even worried about it." And just like that everyone went their own separate way. Big J always had a way of not crossing the line when it mattered and I for one was glad that nothing bad happened.

That year in many ways I became a rebel without a cause. As I look back on that time, I believe that I was much like any other young man trying to find his way. By this time, I was not involved in any extracurricular activities. In the past I had been involved with band and different clubs in the community and was even an usher in the church. But now, there was nothing, just the homies. I was clearly beginning to travel a path that was destined to lead me to my demise.

Spring break rolled around that year and I had no plans outside of the norm and that norm was going to Super Soul Night at the skating rink. Super Soul Night at the skating rink was the best thing ever. The cars used to line the street for at least a mile in both directions and you could hear the speakers "bumpin" as you pulled up to the scene. Super Soul Night was the best.

Me and the crew walked in and the place was packed from wall to wall. The music was pumping, and everybody was there. That night seemed magical. It was like everyone was so happy to see each other. We made our rounds to speak to all our friends and "mack" on the young ladies. This night was simply a great night. But as you know, all good things come to an end.

As I was sitting in one of the back corners of the facility a roar erupted from the crowd. This was a sound that I was all too familiar with. As I looked up, I saw the crowd scrambling. Some were running out of the crowd and some were running in. It was a fight. It was a big fight. When the music went off, I could hear the punches landing. This was a fight for the ages.

My friends and I began to make our way to the front entrance, as it was clear that the night was over with as far as Super Soul Night was concerned. As we proceeded to walk out the front door, shots rang out. The parking lot scattered and you could hear the squealing of tires as cars sped out of the parking lot. I turned back to look for Big J and I heard him yell, "GO! GO!" I turned back towards the parking lot and Herb was there to the rescue. He pulled the van up directly in front of us and Bill flung the door open so we could dive in. As soon as we landed in the van Bill slammed the door and told Herb to go. And like a thief in the night, we were out!

You could feel the adrenaline rushing through all of us in the van as we chattered about what just happened. To say we were pissed about our good time ending is an understatement, but the irony is that we were used to these things happening. Often, whenever we went out a fight would break out and every now and then someone would fire some shots into the air. We were to the point that we planned our escapes for these types of circumstances.

As we made our way back to the "village", our neighborhood, our conversation quickly transitioned from the fight to all the young ladies that were there. As teenage boys this conversation was always at the top of our list. These conversations always lasted a while so as we got out the van we stood around and talked and told jokes. Being young we were just planning to stop by the house for a quick moment and hop back in the van and see where else the night would take us. However, on this night things went a little different as I told the group that I was tired, and I was heading home. Everyone else said the same and we all decided to call it a night. I crept into the house, made my way to my room, and dived under the covers.

As we slept the night away, the city remained awake. My brother Corey, T-Tay, Mon, and Victor aka Brother were all together that night in my dad's car. I am not sure what transpired that night and am unsure of all the details, but as I understand it, they all ended up on Morris Street. While there some words were exchanged, I don't know if this was a face to face type situation or if this occurred as they drove by. However, what I do know is that as my brother and his friends were driving down Morris Street a handgun was given to a young man by the name of Kevin and he fired into my dad's car striking Victor (Brother) in the back of the head. As the story is told Brother fell over into Mon's lap. They rushed him to the hospital. His family got there as soon as they could, but Brother was brain dead and on life support.

The next morning, I was awakened by my Uncle Billy telling me that I needed to go check on Big J because his cousin had been killed. At the time, my Uncle was not the most credible of sources as he was toying with drugs and had a history of not making the best decisions. So, I angrily got up thinking to myself that he didn't know what the hell he was talking about. I made my way over to Big J's house and when I walked through the door it became clear that it was true. Brother was gone.

Up until this point in my life I had never experienced anything like this. This was a person that we went to school with, grew up with, and was family in my eyes. As I closed the door, I immediately sat down in the big recliner. I know that there was a lot of conversation going on around me, but I simply spaced out as the reality of the situation sank in. I was hurt and in disbelief.

Throughout my life I have had moments where God would show my things that I didn't fully understand until after they occurred. A few weeks or so prior to Brother's death, Big J and I ran into him while walking down a path in the neighborhood he stayed in. We were just leaving his house visiting with his brother T-Tay, sister Sharon and his mom Connie. As normal we were both excited to see him. We talked for a while and he told us that he was up at Jerry's, a neighborhood corner store, hanging out. During the conversation he started talking about some beef that was going on. We were not surprised by this topic as there always seemed to be some form of action going on with somebody. As we got ready to leave, Big J looked at him and told him that he needed to be careful out here in these streets. Brother, being brother, leaned down and showed us a small gun he had hidden in his socks. As he revealed the gun to us, he exclaimed, "Oh, I'm gonna be alright".

When I saw the gun, my stomach sank, and a sense of fear ran through my body. At this point in my life, guns were normal for me. My uncle and older cousins carried pistols on them all the time. They would even come out to the house and go in the backyard and fire them. They were the ones that taught me how to fire a gun. However, in this case, things were different. There was a genuine sense of a looming darkness. So, as we parted ways, I looked at Big J and said that that was going to be the death of him. Big J looked into my eyes and turned back to Brother and yelled, "Hey, Man be careful out here.". Brother replied with the biggest smile on his face, "I'm telling you, I'm good.". What I know now that I did not know then was that in a few weeks' time my words would become true. That was the last time that I saw Brother alive. Ever since then, I have had this overwhelming guilt that maybe there could have been something that I could have done to change his fate. Maybe if I had shared with him what I shared with Jason maybe things could have been different.

In the days leading up to the funeral, it was clear that this young man's death had rocked the entire community. The pain of his death is something that I believe that everyone that knew him is still trying to get over until this day. I had seen death, but not like this. This was the senseless killing of a young man from our community by another young man who grew up in our community as well. This was not supposed to happen this way.

The day of the funeral is a memory that I don't think I will ever forget. As I pulled up to the funeral, the church's parking lot was overflowing and had cars lined along the street. The shopping center across the street from the church parking lot was nearly full. As we crossed the street, it was clear that the church was at capacity. People were standing on the steps that led inside of the church knowing that they were not going to be able to get in.

As I crossed the street, the sound of Brother's loved one's weeping escaped out the open doors and windows of the church. This sound rocked me to the core. My heart immediately went out to Brother's mom, Connie. I knew that his entire family was going to miss him, but even at that age I knew that there was something inherently wrong about a mother having to bury her child.

It seemed that every step I took towards the church became harder and harder. There were a million and one thoughts racing through my head. My heart was pounding. Then, out of the blue, I heard a familiar voice call my name. It was Big J's dad. Being a kid without a dad in my life or a solid and positive male figure this man was the closest thing I had to a father figure. So, hearing his voice was like being thrown a life raft in the middle of a stormy sea. We stood outside and talked while the funeral was going on. To him it was clear that Brother's death had a clear effect on me, but his upbeat spirit allowed the pain to subside, if only for a little while.

To say this moment in my life was a turning point for me and my friends is an understatement. In hindsight it was clear that the group of friends began to go in two different directions. One group of friends began to talk about going to college and escaping the city and the second group embraced the streets. Both actions were clearly a way to cope with the pain of losing someone we all loved.

CHAPTER III- FINDING JONATHAN

The school year came to an end and that summer and I enrolled into summer school. Since my family paying for summer school was not an option, I enrolled into a summer program the school system offered that was free of cost. The program offered a construction elective course where the participants received one full credit upon its completion. In short, this was a way to provide free labor for the school system and for poor kids to catch up on their credits. So, this was a win-win for all involved.

It was during this time that I began to really think about going to college again. It had been the start of my freshmen year since this thought had come across my mind. At this point going to college was not about anything relating to academia or the pursuit of a career. It had everything to do with me escaping Statesboro. Since the college prep debacle, my plan was to go to the military. However, now, college was back on the table. And it was a possibility because I managed to keep my math courses on the college level track.

When the following school year rolled around, I was ready. Even with me going to summer school, I still had not acquired enough credits to be in my right grade, but I could see the light at the end of the tunnel as it relates to graduation. By now, I was not as ashamed going to the sophomore homeroom because I saw it as a part of the process of graduating with my class. I knew that all I had to do was pass all my classes and I would be walking with the class of 1992.

This was the year that I learned that just because things don't go as planned doesn't mean that they will not workout. How did I learn this? I learned this by spending what seemed to me the bulk of my junior year in in-school suspension. Don't worry, I didn't kill anyone or had any major disruptive behaviors in school. I was just habitually late for class. That's right, I was in in-school suspension for tardiness. Believe it or not, me being in and out of in-school suspension that year was the best thing that could have possibly happened to me. Coach Hill, the basketball coach, and a teacher whose name was Ms. Brown literally changed my life.

I didn't know what to expect when I first arrived there. I looked around the room and the room were filled with these cubical like fixtures with desks in them. The room was extremely quiet and everyone that was there seemed to know what to do. As I sat down at my desk, Ms. Brown came around and passed out our work packets for the day. In these packets were all the items we needed to complete from our classes. Once we completed these items, we could put our heads on our desks.

Each day I came to in-school suspension I was normally done with all my work by 10:00 am. Shortly after then we went to lunch and I slept for the rest of the day. This was my ritual. This was what I looked forward to everyday that I was there. Then one day that all came to an end.

As normal, I came in and got straight to work. I sat there zipping through all my work assignments and was plotting on the sleep I was about to get. I would glance up at the clock periodically to make sure that I was maintaining my schedule. Well, as fate would have it, Ms. Brown had taken notice of my schedule. This was interesting because up until this moment we had not had much interaction beyond her passing out the packets of class assignments.

The time came for me to turn my work in and it was a few minutes before lunch. I made my way to the basket and dropped off my work. I got back to my desk and laid my head down and closed my eyes and embraced the idea of the sleep I was about to get. Then out of the blue there was a tap on my shoulder. It was Ms. Brown. Normally, the only time I received this tap was when it was an additional assignment that I needed to take care of or if there was a need for me to run an errand for the teachers. Well, this day was different. In a very calm and quiet voice she said, "Why don't you read this book". As she handed me the book, I could see that it was old and tattered. The front cover was worn and torn. The book was black and red and half of the face of the man on the front cover was torn off. I took the book from her and read its title. It was the Autobiography of Malcolm X. Up until this point, I had only heard of the name of Malcolm X in passing through conversations with my uncle.

To please Ms. Brown, I told her that I would read the book. I began reading the book and figured that I would read up until the time came for us to go to lunch and then get back to my normal routine afterwards. I started reading the first few pages until it was time for lunch. It was slow and dry. Nonetheless, when I returned from lunch, I continued to read the book.

The next day I came to class with the same routine in mind. However, when I finished up my work, I figured I would read a few more pages before lunch and get back to my sleep routine when we returned. When we returned from lunch, I found that my interest in this man's story had intrigued me enough to want to continue to read more of the book. As the days passed, instead of finishing my work to go to sleep, I was now finishing my work so I could continue reading this book.

This was the first time that I had read anything about anybody that looked like me that was not Martin Luther King Jr. This was the first time that I finally read something that could articulate what it was like being Black in America. It seemed that every word in this book jumped off the page and provoked thoughts that awakened a spirit inside of me that I didn't know existed. I began to ask questions about myself and my role in this world.

His bravery and ultimately his death gave me the courage to begin to live a life that was dedicated to something that was greater than myself.

When I finished reading the Autobiography of Malcolm X, a thirst to learn more about the Black experience and its role in America began to grow inside me. I started reading everything that I could put my hands on. I was reading everything from W.E.B Dubois to King. I read books about the Civil Rights Movement and Slavery. I read books about the African Diaspora. I read books on social protest and non-violence. By the time my third year in high school ended there was a clear difference between the person that I was at the beginning of the year and the person that I had become.

That summer, my friend Herb came up with the idea that he, I and Stephanie were going to take over the leadership of the Afro-American Club. Prior to this point, I had not been a part of any clubs or activities since my freshman year. It was a novel idea that we would take over the leadership of a club that I had never been a part of and take it to the next level. We spent days planning all the things that we would do if we were able to become the club's new leadership. We literally spent the summer visiting friends' houses and persuading them to get involved with AAC and to vote us in as the club's new leadership.

When my senior year rolled around, I was ready for it. I was officially a part of the graduating class of 1992. For the first time since ninth grade I was in the correct homeroom. Contrary to my ninth-grade teacher's prediction, not only was I on track to graduate, I was going to graduate with my class. And to make things even sweeter, the plan Herb set out on worked. We were the newly elected leadership for the Afro-American Club. He was the president. I was the vice president. Stephanie was the secretary. It was not an easy win, as there were people that had been a part of the club for a while running, but we managed to squeak it out. After the initial meetings, it was discovered that Herb needed to retake a class which made him ineligible to be a participant in the club. So, this was my first introduction to leadership. It was now my responsibility to take on the reigns of implementing the plans that we devised over the summer.

The first thing we had to address was recruitment. Even though Herb was no longer an official member of the organization, he continued to help in executing the plan. We wanted the organization to be the largest club in the school. So, in the mornings we would roam the halls asking people to join AAC. On the weekends, when we saw people out, we would recruit them to become a part of the organization. When the dust settled, we had more than two hundred people in the club and it was not only the largest organization in the school, it was the largest the organization had ever been.

The next thing was to make the organization the coolest thing. So, Herb, being the artist that he was, changed the look of the organization. In the year prior, the club's shirts were jersey styled with numbers on the back. This was pretty much the style for most of the organizations in the school. However, this year, Herb designed a shirt much different. He changed the colors of the shirts from red to purple with black trim. And instead of having numbers on the back, he put the shape of the continent of Africa in the colors of red, yellow, and gold. The idea of the shirts was to symbolize unity and it did, because when the club members showed up to school two hundred strong with these shirts on with their black jeans it sent waves through the school. AAC was here!

Over the course of that year, I began to learn the power of the people. It seemed like there was nothing that we could not do. We created a community choir where we took eighty kids off the streets and gave them something constructive to do. We created a youth step team and held dinners where speakers would come to enlighten us on the latest happenings. We engaged the students and resources at the local university to introduce us to new ideas and experiences. All these things were possible, because we had club advisors that allowed us to explore all our desires.

Ms. Deborah Lee, Ms. Enola Mosely, and Ms. Pricilla Mosley were the advisors for the club. These three Black women were godsends. Whatever idea we came up with they supported it. We planned to take a bus load of students to Atlanta for the annual MLK celebration at no charge to them. They were a little skeptical at first, but after a few successful fundraisers and some lobbying on their part we were able to make it happen.

The trip to Atlanta was amazing. We were able to attend the MLK parade and see all kinds of stars. We had the opportunity to meet Blair Underwood and Jesse Jackson. We also had the opportunity to tour the home of Martin Luther King Jr. and visit the Civil Rights Museum. By this time, I had become somewhat of a history buff, so for me to experience all these things only fueled the fire to learn more for me. While most of the other kids were buying t-shirts and other items, I purchased a book entitled, "A Testament of Hope". The book was a collection of Dr. King's famous speeches and writings. It was right up my alley as by this time I was developing into a public speaker.

Ms. Lee and both Ms. Mosley's were very special to my development as they all brought a special perspective in helping me to understand what it meant to be Black in America. Ms. Pricilla Moseley brought a fiery, don't take no mess perspective. While Enola Moseley was a much calmer woman. Every time you saw her, she always had a smile on her face and was quite upbeat. This taught me to remain forever optimistic. Ms. Lee played more of a consigliere role. She was the one that would hear our grandioso ideas and would walk us through the steps to achieve them.

Of the three, I began to spend much of my time with Ms. Lee in the mornings. I would go to my homeroom and let my teacher know that I was there and then head down to Ms. Lee's homeroom. I spent nearly every morning discussing current and pass events in the news and history and planning the activities for

AAC. We also discussed my plans for college. What I did not know then, but what I have come to realize now is that she was acting as a mentor. She was being that subtle guide for a young man that needed it desperately.

As my senior year was ending, I needed to make some big decisions. I had planned on going to college but had not taken any of the necessary steps to get there. Thank God Ms. Lee had enough insight to steer me in the direction of the Trio program at Georgia Southern University. This was a program at the university that targeted first generation college students. The purpose of the program was to remove any barriers that arise for its students that would prevent them from being successful academically. It was my fortune that this division had a program called Educational Talent Search which was for high school students that wanted to attend college that were facing some challenges.

Educational Talent Search focused on students that were from lower soci-economic backgrounds that desired to go to college. I am not sure how this organization selected its staff, but it did a wonderful job in hiring Renata Newbill-Jallow. By the time I met her, I had already graduated and the only thing that I had accomplished towards my goal of getting into college was taking the SAT. Nonetheless, she walked me through the financial aid and application process to enter college.

To be honest, after graduating from high school, there were only two colleges that I was interested in going to and they were Georgia Southern University and Albany State University. I grew up around Georgia Southern, so it had a natural feel to it, but its major flaw at the time was that it was in Statesboro. At this time, I felt the strong urge to spread my wings and discover the world and get to know who myself.

Then, there was Albany State University which is a Historically Black College/University. I had never been to Albany State University and the only person that I knew that had gone to Albany State was Coach Lee Hill. He would often share his stories of being a student/athlete there with me and a few others when we were sent to in-school suspension. Whenever he spoke of the school he always did so with pride. The only other thing that I knew about the institution was that it was in Albany, Georgia and that city was a place where Dr. King and the Civil Rights Movement had a significant impact.

The summer of that year the Educational Talent Search Program was offering free college tours for its participants. And as luck would have it, the trip that I was notified of was one that was going to Albany State University. The morning of the trip I had a serious case of the butterflies. When I arrived at the office of Educational Talent Search, I knew that when I got on that van it was the start of a new chapter in my life. As I stepped onto the bus, I saw a familiar face. It was my buddy Chief from high school. Seeing him helped to ease the nervousness of the trip and the moment. It seems that there is always something reassuring about a familiar face when you are going into uncharted territory.

The first stop of the trip was a small Georgia Baptist college named Brewton-Parker. The school is in the small town of Mt. Vernon, Georgia. It is a little more than an hour's drive from Statesboro along some rural yet scenic routes through the Georgia countryside. When we arrived, I looked around the campus and I did not feel any connection to this small yet beautiful campus. I just didn't feel a sense of belonging. The staff members that we met were extremely nice and professional, but there seemed to be no connection to me or any of the other students that came with us. We felt as though the staff members were simply checking the boxes on their to-do list so they could get back home to their families on this early Saturday morning. This was a campus tour that felt like it could not end fast enough.

When the tour ended, we all jumped on the bus and began our journey towards Albany, Georgia. We were a little less than two hours away from Albany State University so most of us decided to catch a little sleep on the way. When I awoke, we were nearly there, and the butterflies returned to my stomach. There was an excitement about seeing the place where Dr. King had spent a good deal of time fighting for social justice and equality.

As the van entered the campus and found a parking spot, I gazed at the palm trees as they blew in the gentle breeze. When I stepped off the van it seemed like that day was one of the most beautiful days that God could have created. The sun was shining, and the spirit of the campus was light and inviting. As the students walked by our van, they seemed so happy and full of positive energy. I immediately began to feel a connection to the campus and felt that this was the place for me.

We began to tour the campus and chatter amongst ourselves nervously as the butterflies had yet to fade away. The campus was larger than Brewton-Parker, but it was nowhere near the size of Georgia Southern University. The campus was well maintained. The grass was immaculate, and the tour guide was able to share so much history about the University and the city. One of the stories he shared was the story of how the school was founded based on a chapter in a book W.E.B Dubois wrote called the "Souls of Black Folk". In this chapter in the book, DuBois took a deep look at the trials that African Americans faced in southwest Georgia. Unknown to the guide at the time, if there ever was a sale pitch to close the deal for me, this would be it as Dr. Dubois was and is a hero of mine.

At the end of the tour, the guide asked the group if any of us were interested in becoming Golden Rams and I raised my hand. He took us to the admissions office, and we began to review our admittance information. For some members of the group this was the first time that they had submitted their information to Albany State, but that was not the case for me. This was one of the two schools that I had applied to so when it came time for me to sit with the admissions counselor, I was able to get an on the spot decision. And the decision was clear, I was now officially a Golden Ram!!!

The three-hour trip home seemed to zoom by. I was so excited during the ride home. The adrenaline was racing through my body because I was now officially a college student. Who would have ever thought that this poor kid from the village would ever attend anyone's college? I could not wait to get home to tell everyone, especially my Mom, Grandmother, and Granny. They have always been the ones that believed in me unconditionally and now I could tell them that I was the newest member to the "Ramily".

The day finally came for me to leave for college. The night before I packed everything that I thought I needed for this new chapter in my life. I packed all my clothes, the covers for my bed, my radio, and all my hygiene products. Everything that I owned fit into a suitcase and a trunk. The next morning, I threw it all into the trunk of my Grandmother's car and was ready to go. As I was getting into the car, I heard my mom say in a low tone that Granny was crying. I paused to look up onto the porch where she was sitting and saw a single tear stream down her left cheek. My heart sank as I have always believed that her sole purpose in life was to take care of me, and that when I left home it would not be too long there after that she would die. I went back onto the porch and kissed and hugged her as tight as I could. I whispered to her that I loved her more than she would ever know. Then returned to the car and drove away.

I drove the bulk of the three-hour trip to Albany. It seemed like we, my mom, aunt and I, traveled through a thousand small towns to get there. Nonetheless, we arrived on the Campus of Albany State nearly three hours after our departure from Statesboro. When I arrived on campus I immediately went to my dorm. I was assigned to McIntosh Hall. This was the dorm that the athletes stayed in and the overflow from the freshman dorm. I went into the dorm's office where Brogale was awaiting the arrival for all the students that were assigned to his dorm. I signed off on the paperwork and was sent to room 305.

I made my way up the stairs and unlocked the door to my new

residence. It was a small room with no air conditioning. My roommate had yet to arrive, so I had the pick of which side of the room I wanted. My mom and aunt helped me get everything organized. My mom, seeing that there was no air conditioning, suggested we go to Roses Department store to buy a fan. We made our run to Roses and grabbed the fan and a few more items. They drove me back to the campus, said their goodbyes and handed me forty dollars. Before leaving, my mom looked my square in the eyes and said, This is what you wanted to do so you are going to have to figure it out." as she jumped into the car to head back to Statesboro.

I went back to my room and stood there in silence. My heart was beating fast and the adrenaline was pumping through my veins. I was officially on my own and off at college. This was real and there was no turning back. I walked over to the window as the sounds from the chatter of excitement from below seeped into my room. As I looked out into the sea of strange new faces, I saw a familiar one standing beside a large oak tree in front of my dorm. It was Chief. I nearly leaped for joy. In a loud whisper, I called his name. As he looked up, I could see the joy come over his face as he saw me leaning from the window. He took off like a lightning bolt and ran upstairs. And just like that, the freshman duo was born.

Honestly speaking, I don't know what my freshman year in college would have been like if it was not for Chief. We did everything together. Where you saw one, you saw the other. Whether it was eating lunch, playing basketball, or hanging out with friends we did it together. We were your stereotypical freshman guys. We wanted to be at all the parties and all the happening events.

My first few weeks in school was like sensory overload. Coming from a small rural college town like Statesboro, to attending a historically black college was truly a different world. In my hometown I rarely saw African Americans in key positions. When I went to school, many of the teachers and principals were White. Most of the "smart" kids were White. All the people in the community with power were White. That was not the case for Albany State and Albany, Georgia.

Coming to Albany State allowed me to see African Americans in a totally new perspective. The smartest kid in class looked like me. The professors looked like me. The president of the school looked like me. This was extremely powerful to me. Up until this point in my life, most of the people that I saw that looked like me either worked low waged jobs that kept them in poverty, hustled, or were at best a preacher or teacher. Coming to Albany State allowed me to see first-hand that I could possibly have a future that I could control.

I was able to immediately adjust to college life socially. However, I lacked the academic discipline and skill sets to excel academically. It took my entire first quarter to figure out that I needed to study beyond that of the classroom hours and my grades reflected it. My writing was so bad that I had to repeat the developmental writing course. And I either failed or barely passed every other class. It was bad.

At the beginning of the winter quarter I knew that I was ready. I had the entire Christmas break to get my head together and focus on the mission at hand. When I returned to campus, I was a man on a mission. I kicked off the first few weeks of class with great attendance and I was truly focused. I was getting the work done and my confidence was growing in leaps and bounds. I was finally finding my collegiate academic groove.

February rolled around and I was asked to come back to my hometown and give a speech at an annual dinner that AAC held every year. It felt good to be able to do this because this was an organization that helped me to develop my leadership skills and it was now my turn to act as a mentor. Prior to heading back to Statesboro, I had gotten word that granny was in the hospital. This was nothing out of the norm for me as she has been in and out of the hospital periodically my entire life. It was never anything too serious and she always bounced back like a champion.

On this occasion she was in the hospital in Metter, GA. Metter is a small town about twenty minutes outside of Statesboro. It was also one of the small towns that I had to go through on my way home from Albany. So, on my way to Statesboro to give the speech, I stopped by the hospital to see her. When I walked into the room to see her, I had an unexplainable joy. I was so happy to see her that tears welled up in my eyes and the feelings were the same for her. It was like we had not seen each other in decades. I sat and talked with her a good while and eventually got back on the road to get to Statesboro. As I walked out the door the feeling struck me that this was going to be the last time that I was going to see her alive. And as this thought rendered, my heart sank into my stomach. For the first time in my life, the thought of life without Granny entered my mind.

I made it to Statesboro and gave the speech. I got back on the road and made my way back to Albany. In the days following it seemed that there was just a strange feeling that I could not shake. I tried to pretend that everything was normal, but it was not. On the night of February 25, 1993 granny was on my mind heavily. It seemed that I could not shake the thought of her. As I laid in bed that night, I eventually drifted off to sleep after a long struggle to do so. That night something occurred that had never happened before. I dreamed about granny. It was not a long dream or a dramatic dream. It was a dream of an image of her sitting in a chair with a sad look in her eyes with a single tear running down her face.

When I woke up the next morning my heart was racing as I jumped up and sat on the edge of my bed. I knew that something was wrong. I knew, without anyone telling me that granny was gone. I picked up the phone and called home. The voice on the other end belonged to my uncle Billy. As he was saying hello, I told him that I was on my way home. He responded by telling me that I needed to do just that. I knew then, without any doubt, that my intuition was true. Granny was gone.

I caught a ride home with my good friend Tarrie and another friend of hers. They both lived in a small town not too far from Statesboro called Claxton. When we arrived in Claxton, Tarrie and I were dropped off at her house. When we arrived my mother and cousin Lyn were there waiting for me. I loaded my stuff in the car and jumped into the back seat. My mom asked Tarrie if it was okay for her to get a glass of water. While in the house, my mom shared with Tarrie that granny had passed and let her know how close she and I were. She also explained that I did not know at the time and would not be returning to Albany with them. My mom walked swiftly out of Tarrie's front door with Tarrie close behind her. My mom jumped into the car and Lyn quickly pulled off. I turned to peer out of the back window and saw Tarrie standing in the middle of the street crying. I asked Lyn to stop the car. That is when my mom very calmly told me that Granny was gone.

This was the first time that I had heard the words that the woman that had taken care of me since I was a newborn was gone. In a rush of emotion, I broke down into tears and my heart was shattered into a million pieces. I had never known a hurt like this. I managed to pull myself together as we made the twenty-minute ride over to Statesboro. When I walked into the house, the eerie silence of a packed room permeated throughout the living room. Everyone in the family was looking to see how I was taking the news. I put on a bold face so that everything could have a sense of normalcy, but on the inside, I was destroyed.

The day of her funeral came, and it seemed so surreal. The cars packed the yard as family members and friends prepared to make the long trek to Antioch Missionary Baptist Church. We were all dressed in black. My uncle and older cousins had their customary shades to cover the tears in their eyes. It seemed that the thirty-minute drive, that I had taken a million times before, would never end. When we arrived, I walked into the church and found a seat. As I sat there, I just stared at the casket, the flowers, and the family with the reality of the situation not settling in on me.

Big J and I sat beside each other in church. Granny was like a mother to both of us. As we sat there and listened to the moans of a mourning family it was clear what she meant to everyone. However, during all this pain, an overwhelming surge of joy rushed through my body. I sat there smiling as the woman who had given me everything laid in a casket. At this point it was clear that I was truly a broken soul that did not have the ability to properly process the pain that I was feeling.

When the funeral came to an end and we had buried her, I felt the need to get back to Albany. A few days later, on the trip back to school, I can remember thinking to myself that there was no need to ever go back to Statesboro. I believed that things were never going to be the same as she was the one thing that truly anchored me to the city.

In the weeks and months following granny's death I tried to carry on like everything was normal, but it was not. I finished my first year of school with less than mediocre grades. When I returned home for the summer my grandmother had planned a trip for us to go up to New Jersey. It was a great trip, but the entire time that I was there I was just a shell of a person. The only thing I really wanted to do was get back to Albany to get away from everything that reminded me of Granny.

The summer came to an end and I went back down to Albany. When I returned to the campus, I discovered that I didn't have any on-campus housing. So, over the next few weeks, I stayed with my good friend Pierre until I was able to find a place.

I eventually ended up moving in with my cousin Enika and her mom. They lived in a nice neighborhood on the northside of the city. It was a great place to retreat to when I left campus and it allowed me to be around Enika more. She was a great influence that seemed to be wise beyond her years. She was easy to talk to and one of the most honest people I have ever met.

Being around her was a positive experience. She was smart, positive, and had this can-do spirit about herself. In the mornings she would drop me off on campus and head out to do her daily activities. I really enjoyed these morning trips as I was learning so much about her and her side of the family. I had the opportunity to meet her grandparents on her mother's side. Enika, like them, was planning to become an educator.

Enika and I had a great relationship. However, I never got the feeling that I was fully welcomed by her mother. I never could put my finger on why we didn't mix well, but I always felt that she looked down on me because I came from a poor background. Her family was a solidly middle-class family, but in conversations with her dad it was clear that he had worked for everything that he had. You would think that she would have been a supporter of a young man with good intentions, but I guess not.

In February of 1994, around my birthday, Herb and two other friends had come down to visit me. This was a great visit, as always when Herb came around. Herb needed to take a shower so I invited him over to the house so he could wash up and I could change clothes as well. Well, when we arrived no one was home. So, I asked our two female friends to sit in the living room while we got dressed. At the time, I didn't see anything wrong with it, but in hindsight, I can see how this would be an issue. Nonetheless, Enika's mom came home and all hell broke loose. She went in on me saying that I had all of these strangers in her house, mind you, one of the young ladies was someone that I was seeing at the time and had been over several times previously and she knew well. She continued to go on until the point that I just exploded.

I was in no shape or form a disrespectful person, but I let her know that I knew that she did not want me there. This event triggered all the pent-up pain that was lying dormant inside of me. I began to cry uncontrollably and called out for Granny. The pain was unbearable amid my tears I began to pack up my belongings. It was horrible.

Enika came home and it was clear that she could hear what was going on from the outside. She rushed into the house and came straight to my room. She asked what was going on, but I could not respond. I could not look at her. The only thing I could do was cry and pack. Seeing that I was unable or unwilling to talk she rushed down the hall screaming what did you do towards her mom. She went back and forth down the hall looking for answers, but I quickly finished packing and escaped with my friends. Since then I never had the opportunity to tell Enika how much she meant to me during that time but let the record show that she unknowingly saved me from me.

After this event, I stayed with Chief and his roommate Marvel for a short period. I continued to try to go through the motions of being normal, but the pain from granny's death felt almost new again. I was still going to class, but my work was not the same. I tried to hang out with friends, but that too was not the same.

One day while I was on campus in the student union, my home girl Shonnie walked up to me and asked if I was still staying with Chief. I told her yes and she asked if I wanted to move in with her. Knocking the softball out of the park, I said yes. We went back over to the apartment. Until this day I can't tell you who was packing the fastest, Shonnie or me. My days of sleeping on the couch had come to an end and a new chapter had begun.

When I reflect on this time, I am reminded of the movie "Legends of the Fall". The movie stars Brad Pitt. Tristan, the main character suffered the loss of his brother and carried the guilt of his death. For a few years Tristian dealt with the pain of his brother's death by traveling the world and going into long periods of time away from his family. I, in many ways, went into a period much like this. My trips home became fewer and fewer. As a matter of fact, I began to spend my thanksgivings and Christmases in Albany alone in a small apartment on the eastside of the city.

It was during this hurt filled state that I began to look to external ways to ease the pain. I began to go out more, but I was never really the clubbing type. I didn't drink and was totally against drug use. However, I, like many others, found my vice. Women. During this time, I had been dating a young lady for several years, but in this hurt filled state I pushed her away. It was nothing that she had done, but me recognizing that I was not going to be any good for her. After the break-up it got bad. I began to sleep all day and stay up all night. I stopped going to class and roamed the streets all night. As I look back, I don't even recognize the person that I had become during that period. It is said that hurt people hurt people. I have found this statement to be so true, but what I think it misses is that fact that this includes themselves.

While I was going through this phase of my life, I met Tee. Tee was a proud native of Albany and one of the best people you could possibly meet. He and I became close and over time he has proven to be a great friend. No matter how irresponsible I was being during this time he always allowed me to grow through it without any judgement. I could go through a long list of the good times he and I have had over the years, but there is one experience that he and I will always be joined at the hip with.

I met Tee at the YMCA where I worked on a part-time basis. We would meet up there and tell jokes along with our friend Darren who was one of my co-workers. Darren was about six feet five inches, but he was a gentle giant. When we all hung out, we would talk about the three of us meeting up out outside of the YMCA. Shortly after I left the YMCA, we all agreed to go to a comedy show that was coming to town.

The night of the comedy store was such a magical night. The comedian Earthquake was in town and the city seemed like it was on fire. Everyone was talking about going and we made sure that we had our tickets.

We decided to meet over at my apartment as I lived on that side of town. While there, Tee and Darren had a few drinks. Shortly thereafter, we all jumped in my car and headed to the show. When we arrived at the theater it was jam packed. We ended up parking a block or two away from the facility and made our way back up the street to the theater. When we arrived there, it seemed like everyone was so happy and the spirit in the air was as light as a feather.

We made our way into the theater and went up to the second level. Our seats were in the balcony area which is my favorite place to see a show. When we reached the second level, I saw Nicole, a young lady that I had been spending some time with, along with her friends. Nicole and I had met our freshman year in college and dated for a short time, but we ended up going our separate ways. I had recently started talking to her again, so I went over and spoke to her and her friend. Tee, Darren, and I then made our way to our seats. By chance, we ended up sitting next to one of Tee friends and we ended up laughing and joking with them through the entire show. I don't know what it was, but it seemed like everything that came out of each comedians' mouth was hilarious.

The show ended and we felt that we had all gotten more than our money's worth. As we were exiting the show, we decided to use the main exit instead of using the exit nearest the street that we were parked on. As we pushed the door open it seemed that the entire crowd that was on the inside just stopped and had a reunion right in front of the building. From the crowd I heard a familiar voice scream out, "My Baby!". It was Nicole. She quickly ran up to me and buried her head into my chest while hugging me as tight as she could.

I smiled and hugged her back, but suddenly things seemed to begin to move in slow motion. I held my head up and looked into Tee's eyes. They were wide with excitement as he began moving towards me. I, being in an altered state, began to push Nicole away from me. I looked at her friend Jennifer and told her to get Nicole out of there. Then, simultaneously, I felt my right arm being lifted into the air while Tee was brushing past me. I turned and saw that it was the young lady that had recently broken up with several months ago. Filled with anger, she screamed to the top of her lungs," Anybody, but her!" knowing that Nicole and I's past relationship had casted a shadow on ours. Being young, we argued for a bit and went our separate ways.

Tee, Darren, and I got back into the car and made our way back to the apartment. When we got there the Tee and Darren's jokes on me were never ending. Tee and Darren sat there laughing and drinking coke with Paul Masson. I didn't mind as everything was said and done and we were home safe. Then there was a knock at the door. It was Nicole. She came for clarification and wanted to know whether I was still seeing the young lady. I told her no and reassured her that I was not seeing anyone else at the time. As she got ready to leave, she vicariously mentioned that she was going out with her friends that night. I thought this was odd as she never went out, but hey!

Darren, Tee, and I continued with the jokes and ESPN. A couple of hours had passed, and we had not left the living room of my apartment. Then the phone rang. It was my friend Daryl. Speaking with his unique Florida accent I heard him say, "Look here my nigga. You better get down here fast as you can, because your old lady is following Nicole around the club trying to fight". We jumped in the car, sped out of the parking lot and was heading to the House of Jazz. When we had arrived, I could hear the voices say, "There go Jay Right there". I searched through the crowd and saw neither of them there. I jumped back in the car and raced over to Nicole's apartment. When I got there, she was upstairs in her bed. She was pissed, but not at me just the situation. We talked for a little while and me and the guys left.

That night was surely a rollercoaster for all of us. What we didn't realize was how that night was going to have such an impact on our lives. When it ended, we all agreed that we had to hang out again, so we decided that we were going to hang out that Saturday.

That Saturday came and I was ready to go. I knew Darren had to open the gym that morning, so I decided to give him a call a little bit after noon. I gave him a call and his roommate picked up the phone. I asked to speak to Darren and there was a long pause. The voice on the other end said, "Jay you don't know do you?" I replied, "Know what?" Darren's roommate went on to tell me that Darren had laid across his bed that morning and died from a massive heart attack. I stood in the kitchen with the phone in my hand in a state of shock. How could this be true? We were just together less than forty-eight hours ago. How could he be gone?

When I broke the news to Tee, he was in disbelief. The look on Tee's face clearly communicated that he was shook by the news. The only thing that we could talk about was the fact that we were just with him and how much fun we had together.

The day of Darren's funeral arrived, and Tee and I were still in shock. Tee came by the house and we rode to the funeral together. It was a large funeral in a large church that was packed to capacity. As I sat there, I believed that this funeral was going to be much like the funerals that I had attended in the past, but it was not.

I don't know the minister's name that gave Darren's eulogy, but it was a message that I would never forget. In his message he talked about the Greek god Kairos. In his eulogy he explained that Kairos was the Greek god of opportunity. He went on to describe Kairos as being bald with a ponytail on the front of his head. He also stated that the only way to grab Kairos was to catch him by the ponytail as he came on the scene, because if you tried to catch him as he was leaving your hand would slip off of his bald head. The essence of his message was that Darren had lived his life and now it was up to us to take advantage of this gift called life. It was now our time to seize the opportunities that have been laid before us as we do not know when we will take our last breath.

In the time following Darren's death, the desire to do more and be more was awakening in me. Up until this point I have always considered myself conscious of the matters around me, but now there was a new element that was added to the mix and it was the understanding that every day that we are alive is an opportunity to make ourselves better and to help others around us. However, along with this understanding I knew I had to gain some stability in my life. I was close to two hundred miles away from home and my family could not afford to support me. Besides, I had gotten older and understood that I needed to become more financially secure. The only problem with this was that I wanted to take the hare's approach versus being that of the tortoise.

By this time, I was working more than I was going to school. I had obtained a fulltime job at the local Wal-Mart vision center as a sales associate. The money was not the best, but it was the most that I had ever made up until this point in my life. I stayed there for about two years and was offered a position with a local ophthalmologist.

When I began work with Dr. Dixon I was truly inspired by his story. He was originally from one of the islands in the Caribbean and had come to the States to pursue his education. What was so inspiring about his story was all the sacrifices that he made to become a doctor. In one of his stories about this journey, he explained to me that while he was in medical school, he and his wife were so broke that they lived in an apartment with no furniture or beds in it. And while he was going to class and studying, his wife was working a low wage job to make the ends meet. Dr. Dixon said that at this point in their life the only things that they really owned were the clothes on their backs and the pots and pans that they used to cook their food.

The hard work and sacrifices paid off for them. While I was working with Dr. Dixon, he had his first year where he made a million dollars. They no longer lived in an apartment, but a beautifully custom-built home and they both drove very nice cars. They were now the parents of two very beautiful children and pillars in the community. Through a short period of sacrifice, he and his wife were able to build a foundation that now their family and greater community was able to benefit from.

It was while I was working for Dr. Dixon that I realized that I had to put myself into a position to take care of myself, my family, and the ones I loved. It did not matter how well intentioned or conscientious I was if I did not have the means to secure a stable financial foundation. So, in all my wisdom, I devised a plan. I decided that I was going to finish my degree, earn my realtor's license, get a second job, and open a car wash. And yes, I attempted to do all these things at the same time.

I ultimately ended up resigning from Dr. Dixon's office and began to substitute teach as I was working to complete my degree, wash cars, and push buggies at the local Sam's club. By this time, my oldest son was born so my fire to do more was there, but what I didn't realize at the time was that I was doing a lot, but not completing anything. And as a result, when it came time for me to take my final exam in the real estate course, I bombed it and the car wash business ultimately ended up failing.

What I learned through this process was that there was so much that I did not know when it came to finances. In fact, I was completely ignorant. Growing up, the only thing I knew was to pay your bills, put food on the table and be thankful if you were able to do both. The idea of saving a little each month was foreign because everything was so hand to mouth. And by the time you had any extra money, you just wanted to celebrate not being broke.

I went through a stage where I wanted to do the most, but it seemed like everything was ending in failure. Then to make matters worse, I ended up being in a pseudo state of homelessness. I had given up my apartment to move in with the mother of my son, but our relationship didn't work out. So, I had to move out and ended up staying a short while with Tee's mom, Ms. Harris. She was about as sweet of a person you could ever find, but my pride would not let me stay there. So, I ended up staying with my friend Rick and his sister Kee-Kee.

These were some of the most depressing days of my life. Up until this point, I always had something positive going whether it was school or work. Now, it was nothing. I had no job, no car, no money, and a son that I was failing to be able to provide for. Each day felt like groundhog's day. I would wake up and play Tetris all day and wait for Kee-Kee to cook. Every now and then some of the folks that I hung out with in the past would stop by as we were all mutual friends. I would hear them snickering as I knew that I had become the butt of the joke. Polo wearing, fresh car driving Jay was now reduced to the guy that slept on a couch.

So, after a period of feeling sorry for myself, I decided that I had to make a move. Whenever I found myself in situations like these I would reach out to good friends and seek advice. Well, in this case, I reached out to Big Jay. I told him about the situation that I was in and how I was living. As it turned out, he was in a tight situation himself, but as normal we always found a way to find some humor in whatever it was that we were going through. During the conversation he was able to suggest I didn't necessarily want to hear, but it was what I needed to do. And the suggestion was to move back to Statesboro.

The entire time that I had been away from Statesboro I put into my mind and spirit that I was never going to move back to that town. I often said that if I ever moved back to Statesboro then that meant that I had failed. Then in a moment of reflection it occurred to me that if sleeping on someone's couch and waiting on them to feed me was not a sign of failure then I was never going to know what one was.

Big Jay's suggestion was solid, and I knew that this was the best option for me. I knew that if I got back home then I could enroll into Georgia Southern University and finish my degree. The only problem that I had now was that I didn't have a way home. Then out of the blue Big Jay said that he had ran into Kenya, a childhood friend, while he was in Statesboro a while back. And by chance, he had gotten her number. Hearing this was like manna falling from the heavens. He gave me the number, so I gave her a call when we hung up.

Growing up I had a close circle of friends. We were loyal to each other and there was pretty much nothing we would not do for each other, right or wrong and regardless of the circumstances, and Kenya was a part of this circle. So, I knew when I called her that she would come to Albany to pick me up.

When I called Kenya, she picked right up as expected. She told me to hold on as she was checking out of the hospital. Now this was not unusual for Kenya as she has sickle cell and was routinely in and out of the hospital. She got back on the phone with her normal jokes stating that she was checking out of her favorite spot. I laughed with her a little and then told her I needed for her to come pick me up. She told me that she was too weak to drive that distance, but she would let someone else drive her car down to Albany. We thought about it for a while and came up with Bill.

Now Bill was a notorious liar in the group. So, when I gave him a call, I knew that this conversation could go in any direction. I told him that I needed for him to ride with Kenya to Albany to pick me up. He said that he would do it and for me to call him back when she was ready. I felt funny when I hung up the phone with him as I knew then that I was not going to see him. When I called back, he never picked up the phone. I was pissed about this as his lies always had bad timing.

I called Kenya and the next name that came to mind was Danny. Danny had been a longtime friend that was established more so than the rest of us. By this time, he had opened some businesses in the Statesboro community and was doing well. He was a guy that busied himself with hustling and making money. So, when I called him, I figured he would be busy, and yes, he was. However, he could sense in my voice that I was desperate. So, he dropped what he was doing, met up with Kenya, and took off to come pick me up in Cordele, Georgia which was about thirty minutes from Albany. While they were on route, I was tasked with finding a ride to meet them.

I gave my boy Carl a call as I knew I could depend on him to take me there. In Albany had built a solid reputation as being a person that would go beyond the call of duty to help a friend. In the case of Carl, I believed that I had shown myself to be more than a good friend. He and I had become roommates at one point. When he moved in the only thing, he had to do was bring his things as the first month's rent and deposit was paid. I recognized that he was a good guy in a tight situation, so it was what it was as far as I was concerned.

While rooming together, Carl managed to find a job that was in Cordele, but he didn't have any reliable transportation, nor did he feel that he had the appropriate clothing to look professional in while on the job. So, I let him drop me off at work and wear some of my clothes so he could get back and forth to work and look the professional part for the job. So, you can only imagine the shock I felt when he told me that he wasn't going to take me to meet up with my ride back to Statesboro. I recall telling him that if the roles were different that I would do it for him without hesitation. And his response was something that I would never forget. He said, "Lil Jay just because you would do this for someone else doesn't mean that they will do it for you". In that moment I learned a valuable lesson that follows me until this day. Every kind deed that I do is repayment for every little bit of favor that God has shown me.

Suffice it to say that when I got off the phone with him, I was more than pissed. I had Kenya and Danny on the way to meet me and I had no way to get to Cordele to meet them. I didn't want to ask Rick and Kee-Kee, even though I knew they would have done it, because they had helped me so much thus far. Frustrated, I walked over to my friend's Vega's apartment to get away for a moment.

Vega and I knew each other from campus and hung out from time to time prior to me staying with Rick and Kee-Kee. I would stop by her spot periodically just to talk. She was in a situation where she had gotten pregnant and the father of the child was having a tough time accepting it. I guess in a way we were somewhat therapeutic for each other as I was going through a tough moment with the mother of my son.

When I got over to her apartment, she was busying herself with things in the house and we just started into our normal conversation. I began to tell her about how pissed I was about not having a ride to meet my friends in Cordele and could not understand how a guy that I consider a friend refused to help me after all of the sacrifices I had made for him. She listened for a moment and very calmly said, "I will take you." With these words my heart sank as I was shocked by two things. First, I didn't realize Vega had a car and second her willingness to take me at such a late hour.

I left her apartment and headed over to Rick's apartment feeling as though a burden had been lifted off my shoulders. A little while later she met me at the apartment to pick me up in what seemed to be the latest model Cadillac with all the bells and whistles. As I loaded my stuff into the car, I realized that I only had eight dollars to my name. When I told her that she simply replied that I didn't have to pay her and that she was doing this as a friend. Vega had always been a sweet person and this action really spoke volumes as to the person that she was.

We sat out on the forty-minute drive to Cordele, Georgia. I was filled with uncertainty but was willing to take this step relying on my faith. We arrived in Cordele just before midnight and like clockwork, when we arrived at the McDonald's Kenya and Danny was already there. Seeing their faces was like seeing superheroes arrive to save the day. Danny immediately went to unload my things and pack them into Kenya's car. I said my goodbyes to Vega and snuck the eight bucks into her ashtray. I knew that the money didn't mean anything to her, but I just wanted to let her know how grateful I was for her willingness to bring me to catch my ride home. As I got into the back seat of the car and laid down, like a good friend, Kenya informed me that for the next two and half hours that she was going to be talking shit about my ass. And for me, that is when I knew that I was on my way home.

CHAPTER IV - RETURNING TO THE NEST

To my amazement it felt good to be back home and see all the familiar faces. The love from my family and friends was so real and they were more than happy to get busy with the work of helping Jonathan. I stayed in my childhood home for a few weeks, but after I was accepted into Georgia Southern University, I moved into an apartment that was a little closer to campus.

Transferring from Albany State University to Georgia Southern University was like going to Harvard for me. Even though this university was in my hometown, the cultural shock was real. I went from attending a school and living in a city, for almost ten years, where mostly everyone looked like me back to the hometown that was still grappling with the idea of diversity in many aspects. However, the difference between me leaving and returning to Statesboro was that I knew who I was.

Enrolling into Georgia Southern University was like getting a new start. When I enrolled at Georgia Southern University, I was close to graduation from Albany State and only needed to complete residency hours to meet Georgia Southern's requirements for completion. As chance would have it, I met Dr. Saba Jallow who was the director for the Center for Africana Studies for the university. From the first time I met this phenomenal man who until this day, acts as a mentor and inspiration for me. So, when it came to deciding what minor I was going to pursue, it was easy to choose Africana Studies.

Up until this point I had a pretty good grasp on the issues that we were facing within the continental United States. However, working with Dr. Jallow opened my mind to the greater matters of humanity and allowed me the ability to translate these issues all the way from the local level to the global scales. I was able to hone these skills by becoming a participant in the Model African Union. In its simplest form the Model African Union is much like the Model United Nations. It was through this experience that I was able to gain a working knowledge of the issues that were facing the continent of Africa and many of its countries.

Every year the Model African Union convenes in Washington, DC for its national conference. Here, students from around the nation and world convened to discuss policies and solutions to the matters that the countries on the African continent are facing. Schools like Penn State, UC Berkeley, University of Miami, Howard University, and many more came to compete in this simulation. You would think that we were solving all the world's problems the way we debated each other. This experience awakened thoughts that were much broader and deeper than before. However, having the opportunity to meet the Ambassadors from these countries had to be one of the most rewarding experiences for me.

It was so amazing to see how these Ambassadors beamed with so much pride as they spoke about their respective countries. They gushed about the beauty of their land and the riches of their natural resources. They were all very inviting as they encouraged us all to one day travel to their homelands. You could feel the energy in the room from all the positivity. When the opening session closed, we all went to our assigned conference rooms to meet with the Ambassadors for the countries that we were representing.

The one-on-one sessions with the Ambassadors were opportunities for the students to get a better understanding of the issues that our respective countries were facing. At the time, I was representing the country of Gabon for Georgia Southern University. Gabon was stable and there were not too many pressing matters that were going to be addressed by the body at large. Well, during this process we had an Ambassador to visit with us from Sudan. When he entered the room, he had a glowing smile that was pretty much shared by all the Ambassadors. He made his way around the room and shook the hands of everyone that was there and then he took his place in front of the room in a chair that had been placed there for him. He started out by telling us about all the glowing attributes his country held within its borders. He discussed the rich caches of oil and all the potential that these caches held. But inevitably we had to open the discussion regarding the conflict in Darfur.

This gentleman gave us a gut-wrenching discussion about the level of poverty and violence that his country was facing. When he began to discuss the horrors that were the result of the conflict in Darfur there was a clear change in his demeanor. He became very solemn. He appeared to almost physically shrink as tears rolled down his cheeks as he described the images of mutilated bodies, destruction, and chaos. To see a man that walked into the room that was filled with regality and pride reduced to tears was a moment that I would never forget as it was in that moment I knew that if anything was going to change about this world then it would have to be the people that would lead that charge. It would be up to us to replace greed with the desire to serve humanity and the greater good.

When I left Washington D.C after the African Union, I was a changed person. Listening to the ambassador fueled my understanding of how important public policy was for those that it is intended to serve and protect. It was also abundantly clear, that when the matters of public service are placed into the hands of the wrong people then it is truly the people that pay the price of incompetence, greed, power fueled narcissism.

The following fall I enrolled into a class that focused on the American Civil Rights era. It was a large class so when I arrived, I typically sat in the back seat near the door. I was familiar with the civil rights era and its major actors. So, I would often sit back and listen to the other students as they discussed their perspectives on the developments of the period.

In this class there was a young White female that stood out to me. She was southern in all aspects of the word. She was also a supremely intelligent young lady that did not shy away from sharing her opinion regarding the things that transpired during this time period. It seemed that in every class period she had a unique point to make on all the readings. However, what seemed to stand out to me about this young lady was that everything that she said seemed to come from a very heady and academic standpoint. It seemed that there was never any connectivity or empathy towards the subject when she discussed it. And for some reason, I was always perplexed by this.

Up until this point, when it came to matters such as social justice and equality, I had primarily been inundated with the voices within the African American community. It seemed that I could count on one hand the number of Whites, or anyone else for that matter, that were fighting to be a voice for those that had gone unheard. Even while on the trip to the African Union, the bulk of the people there were either African American or African. And those that were from other groups, seemed to be there solely for academic reasons. I could never feel their connection to the people that were suffering from these atrocities. Moreover, it seemed as if it was their desire to be recognized for the awards at the conference rather than providing real and heartfelt solutions to the problems for the people of these nations.

This course was pretty much the run of the mill class with some caveats in the professor's perspective of historical events. As this class moved forward through the semester, we were advised that we would be taking a trip to Atlanta to visit the King Center that was showing an exhibit of the lynching of African

Americans. I was not particularly excited as by this time I had visited the King Center on several occasions.

The day arrived when we were to head to Atlanta for the visit. Atlanta is about three hours away so the bulk of the people on the trip either slept, talked softly, or caught up on their school-work. I managed to do a combination of the three. We arrived at the King Center and collected ourselves as the professors for the class went and retrieved the passes for the exhibit. They returned shortly thereafter, and we all made our way into the center. The group made its way through the center corridors and we all engaged the works that were there and had small discussions about the items that were on display. The pieces that they had were very intriguing and once again I was not disappointed by the trip to the King Center.

The group made its way to the entrance where the lynching exhibit was being housed. We formed a line for entry and began to move into the space. As I walked through the line, I began to see these horrific images of mutilated bodies hanging from trees, posts, and the like. Even more disturbing than the pictures were the grotesque stories that were attached to them. Some stories talked about how lynching was part of the social fabric of life and how people would come from miles around to watch them. In some stories it talked about how law enforcement were the ones leading the mob, a fact that I knew to be true as this was the case for the Cato & Reed lynching in my hometown of Statesboro. However, of all the stories the ones that I thought were the more stunning were the ones that discussed how the lynching would be announced in church services and the crowd would flow out from the sanctuary to replace the glow of God with the glow of a Negro being burned at the stake.

I can't put into words the emotions that boiled inside of me as I went from station to station. I could hear the conversation from other students and could even pick up on the quiet whimpering of a few, but what struck me the most I didn't see coming. As chance would have it, I was in line behind the young White female that I mentioned earlier. The flow of the line through the exhibition hall was consistent and moved fairly well. Then I noticed that the young lady began to walk a little slower than the rest of the group. At first, I really didn't think too much of it until I noticed that the gap between her and the person ahead of her was getting larger and larger. Her pace then ultimately ended up in a complete halt. She began to shake her head and repeatedly say that she was so ashamed. I reached out to her to place my hand on her shoulder, but she immediately turned around and fell into my arms. I could feel her body quiver as she cried uncontrollably while repeating the words that she was so ashamed and asking how anyone could do this to somebody. She continued to cry and shake until the point she began to hyperventilate. We carried her to the entrance area of the building and laid her down so she could get some fresh air. She eventually was able to regain her composure. I knew in that space and time that this young lady was never going to be the same and nor was I as this was the first time that I saw a heart break when faced with the atrocities that are a part of the Black experience that was not Black itself. Sometimes the universe places you in a position at a certain time because it is opening your eyes to the fact that we are all connected in the fabric of humanity and that these artificial barriers that we embrace are not the will of God, but the construct of self-serving men.

At this point in my life I had taken a hiatus from dating. I believed that this was a time in my life where I needed to focus on me, completing my degree and getting my life in order. When I had left Albany, I would have been homeless if it was not for the kindness of some good friends. And what I learned from the situation was that I had to get a real handle on my life.

I was living pretty much like a hermit. I went to class, to the gym, and back home. I spent a lot of this time reading and getting to know the person that I had become. I spent a lot of time having conversations with myself and identifying exactly what it was that I wanted out of life. Prior to this moment in my life,

I pretty much lived day to day. Though I was completely aware of the issues that our society was facing and had clear opinions about them all, I had yet found my true voice as I had not truly defined who I was. This moment in my life was a time of personal growth, healing, learning, and detoxing from relationships, both with friends and romantic interests, that were toxic to my soul.

It was during this period that I had become love struck. One day in the gym, near the end of the semester, I saw a young lady playing racket ball with some friends. I saw her from a distance and was not close enough to get a name or introduce myself to her. Even if I was, I don't believe I would have taken the opportunity to say anything.

At the beginning of the fall semester, I was approached by Dr. Jallow with the task of helping him prepare some students for the regional Model African Union. I agreed and we decided to set up a team practice. Well, when the day rolled around for the team practice, I was running a little behind and was rushing to get there. When I arrived and walked into the room where we were practicing, I was immediately struck by a familiar face. It was her. It was the girl from the gym. As we went through the practice, I had to keep my cool and not give her any "special" attention. However, I was trying to be as smooth as possible as I was checking her out.

The team met several times before heading up to Atlanta for the regional Model African Union conference. During the entire time we were meeting, I never said a word to let her know that I was interested, but I did share with some friends that I thought she was "that deal". While at the conference my longtime friend Tee came by to hang out for a while. I swung by the room where she and the rest of the girls were staying so he could see her. As we left, he gave his stamp of approval and we left out to see what the city of Atlanta had offered.

The next day the teams assembled in the conference room for

a short program. Following the program, we all went to our respective meeting areas for our committees. It was during these committees that her mom, who lived in the Atlanta area, had stopped by to observe her while in our committee. She and I served on the same committee. I was the chair and she was the representative for her country. Her mom observed how I ran the meeting and was so impressed that when we went on break, she introduced me to herself and daughter not knowing that we already knew each other. The conference eventually came to an end and we made our way back to Georgia Southern. I don't recall seeing her during the time following the conference, but from time to time she would cross my mind.

The next semester rolled around, and I was ready to go. For the first time I could see that light at the end of the tunnel, and it shined upon graduation. I had been in college for over a decade and I was ready to bring this chapter to a close. So, when the first day of classes started, I was ready to go, but was a little taken aback when I saw that this young lady was in the Model African Union class.

You would think by now I would have said something to her to let her know that I was interested, but I had not. I came to class day after day and did not say a word to her. As the class was preparing to go and be a part of the National Model African Union in Washington DC, the students in the class were tasked with deciding what committee they would like to serve on. Eventually the day rolled around to where we had to let Dr. Jallow know what our decisions were. Well, of all days, Adrianne, the young lady, did not show up for class. So, I, being the caring guy that I was, placed her on my committee and agreed to contact her to catch her up with what was happening with the group.

I gave her a call on a Thursday prior to Valentine's Day weekend to catch her up on what the developments in the class were and to let her know that she was serving on my committee. I explained to her that we would need to get together at some point to work on the resolutions that we had to prepare. Unexpectedly, she said that we could get together this weekend. I was a little taken aback by this as I figured that she would have plans for Valentine's Day. Trying not to look too anxious, I pretended to have plans and told her this weekend was not going to work and that I would follow back up with her. Early the next week I gave her a call to plan for us to hook up to discuss the class work. I went over that evening and we have been together every day since.

CHAPTER V - KILLING JAY

What I have come to understand about life is that there are going to be some good days and there are going to be some bad days, but ultimately you want your good days to outnumber your bad days. And up until this point I was doing battle daily to pay the rent, keep food on the table, finish my degree, take care of two kids, and maintain a relationship. Financially, I was surviving on student loans and whatever work I could find. I did everything from load trucks, to substitute teach, and work for the Boys and Girls Club. I was in complete survival mode.

There were some days where I would wake up and the electricity was turned off or the water would be turned off. The rent was constantly late. Thank God, I had a landlord that was willing to work with me when it came to the rent. This was also a time where my Aunt Betty would bring me food donations from the church so that Adrianne and I would have something to eat. Yes. This was a period that was tough, but what I firmly believed then, as I do now, is that tough times are not meant to last always. And if you are strong enough to weather the storm then you will be better for it in the end.

I can't pretend to know why God puts me into certain situations or not, but what I do concede is that his knowledge and wisdom is infinite. In February of 2004 I went to the mailbox and in it was a letter from Dekalb County asking for me to appear for a hearing for "Child Abandonment". As I read the letter my heart sank. I was perplexed as I had just given a lump sum of funds for my kids. Nervous and unsure, I made the arrangements to appear in court.

This court day is a day that I will never forget. When I walked into the courtroom all I saw was a sea of black and brown faces. My heart rate sped up, but I remained confident that once I went through the process everything would be okay. The judge came into the courtroom and she was visibly pissed. I don't know what happened prior to her taking the bench, but whatever it was she did not like it. She announced to the courtroom that all fines were going up from $1000 to $2500. She went on to state that we could step outside and meet with the representatives from the Child Support office to go ahead and start the process prior to coming before the bench. When she said this, I felt relief as I had already gone down to the local child support office and started the process of taking it out on myself.

She began to call out the names one by one and eventually made it to my name. As I made my way down to stand in front of her, I felt that this was going to be a mere formality and I would be leaving shortly. Saying that I was wrong would be an understatement. I explained to the judge that I had sent money to the mother with the understanding that it was to last until I received my next student loan check disbursement. I also explained I had already started the process of taking child support out on myself. Everything that I told the judge was true and seemingly very logical, but it did not save me. She asked me if I had a receipt for payment and I said no. She looked at me, took a deep breath and called for the bailiff.

I was shaken to my core. I was in disbelief. There I was being handcuffed and about to be hauled away to jail at a point in my life when I was trying so hard to get my life together. For a brief moment, I lost it. I was enraged at the fact that I allowed myself to be put in such a vulnerable situation by not understanding the legal ramifications of having children out of wedlock.

As I sat there handcuffed in the courtroom it seemed that every person that went before the judge eventually made their way over beside me to await their journey to the jail. When the proceedings ended, we were all loaded up onto a van and taken over to the jail for processing. As I stood in the holding cell, I listened to the stories of the men that were there with me.

One of the stories that I was able to hear came from a man that was in his late forties or early fifties. He was just released from prison and had nearly $40,000 in back child support to pay. In our conversation, he said that he had no job, but was able to scrape up forty bucks to pay on the debt that he owed. While in court, when the judge heard this, she immediately called for the bailiff to take him away. Another young guy who was a US veteran that was living out of his car and working temp jobs, shared his story and his frustration with the system. As I sat there and listened to the stories of those that were around me, I quickly began to realize that my situation was not as bad as theirs and it could have easily been a whole lot worse. I, unlike everyone else that was in the cell with me, knew that I was going to be walking out of that facility later that evening. What I did not know was that I was going to be the only one that was in the holding cell that was going to be able to sleep in my own bed that night.

Over the course of the next seven months I traveled back and forth to Atlanta to stand before the court. When I first came before the judge, a middle-aged Asian guy, I was emotionally drained as it related to this matter. The relationship between myself and the mom had progressively gotten worse and it was beginning to take a toll on her and I both. As I stood next to the judge, I believed that he could see that I was having a tough time with this matter, so he began to start a little small talk to lighten my mood. Seeing that I had been assigned a young White female attorney that was a graduate of the University of Georgia's Law School whom he was familiar with, he began to talk about how passionate she was about her work.

It was nearing the time for my case to come up, so we began to bring our conversation to a close. My nerves were beginning to subside, and I think it began to show. He glanced at me and told me to trust the process. It was at this moment that I looked at him sarcastically with the "really? face". He laughed and said, "well just trust me". I told him that I could do that, but he had lost me with the trust of the process part. We went through the proceedings and were assigned another date to return.

Several months later, in October, I was called to come back to court. As I made the long drive up Interstate 16 and 75, I had a sickening feeling sitting in the pit of my stomach. The night before I was restless, and the lack of sleep was taking its toll on me during the drive. When I arrived at the courthouse, I sat there patiently waiting for my case to be called. Meanwhile, my attorney had arrived and began to prepare herself for her argument. Every time I had spoken to her prior to this moment she was somewhat talkative and more engaging. On this day she was not. She was focused and literally sitting on the edge of her seat.

After a few hours the courtroom had emptied some and my name was finally called. As I stood before the bench, my pulse quickened as I watched the judge pour over the information that had been presented to him. As he finished, he read the specifics of the issues that were being addressed by the court. He then looked at the prosecutor and asked, how much did I owe? The prosecutor quickly glanced at me and looked at the judge and said $17.

After hearing this the judge threw his hands into the air and leaned back into his chair and exclaimed loudly, "$17! We are here for $17. This is a gross misuse of the system". He then looked at the prosecutor and asked her, "What do you want me to do with this?" In her delayed response, my attorney quickly jumped in and said, "through it out". The judge looked back at the prosecutor. She nodded her head in agreement and he threw the case out.

In my case, I know that I was extremely fortunate, but the fortune did not translate over to my personal situation. For years, and even until this day, this situation remains difficult.

In hindsight, there are a million things that I wish I had done differently to make this situation better. However, hindsight is always 20/20. But what I can tell anyone that is going through this situation is that if there is an opportunity to work out an agreement between the parents please do. The result will be much better in the long term, but if there seems to not be any foreseeable resolution then please use this as a last resort. The court is not designed to save a family, mend a broken heart, or truly prescribe what is best for a child, but to ensure that there is a fiscal mechanism in place to take care of the child.

For the next ensuing months, I worked a combination of jobs to make the bills meet. For a short time, I worked at the Boys and Girls Club as a counselor in the Teen Center. After a short time there, I got a long-term substitute teacher job at one of the local middle/high schools. After a short time there, I became the head middle school basketball coach for the girls' team. And during all of this I managed to finally complete my degree.

I, like my commencement speaker Andrew Young, knew one thing upon my graduation and that was that I did not know anything. The only thing that I was sure of was that I had to immediately go into graduate school. So, that fall I enrolled into the Averitt School of Graduate Studies at Georgia Southern University in its Master of Public Administration program.

It was around this time that I began to believe that things were turning around for me. I was ending some chapters in my life that had been open for too long. However, I still had a long journey in front of me even with all the progress that I had made. So, there I was enrolled in graduate school, but still looking for a job that could support my family. And then suddenly, like an act of God, there was my opportunity.

One day while out on the job trails, I was informed that the local alternative school was looking to hire a new teacher. Excited to hear this news, I woke up early the next morning and headed to the Board of Education to put my name in the hat for the position. When I arrived, I went in to apply, but was surprised to learn that the job was not at the Board of Education, but with a private company that had taken over the alternative education program for the county. Ms. Dixon, the front desk employee for the county, gave me the address as to where I could find the program. I thanked her and made my way over to the facility.

The center was in a shopping center in the eastern part of the city. When I arrived, it was clear that the center was in disarray. As I approached the door, I could see that the students were up walking around and playing. It was so bad that when I knocked on the door it was a student that let me in instead of a teacher.

The lead teacher came over and I began to inquire about the teaching opportunity with the program. As we spoke, she told me that in fact there was a teaching position available and that I needed to apply via the parent company, Ombudsman. I left my information with her and went home to apply online for the position. A few days later, I traveled down to Hinesville, GA to interview for the position. When I left Statesboro that morning, I was certain that I was going to go interview for a teaching position, but unbeknownst to me, I was interviewing for the director position. Suffice it to say that the interview went great as by the time I reached home I had received a call offering me the position.

To come home with this news was the best feeling ever. I was finally able to get my first professional job with a professional salary of $35,000. For some, making $35,000 is not much, but for me this was the most money I had ever made in my life. And to add to this windfall of cash, I had the opportunity to earn extra money by working during the summers. Finally, me and my family were working our way to having some form of financial security. When I got this job, I thought that the money was the blessing, but I quickly learned that was not the case.

I firmly believe that God puts you where you ought to be when you ought to be there. And this was the case for me as it relates to this job. Prior to this moment I had worked with young people in multiple capacities. I had coached, counseled, mentored, and the more. I believed that up until then I had been a positive influence on many young people, but this time it was my turn to learn something from those that I was supposed to serve.

You will hear me say often that if you want to learn the real issues of a community then go visit its alternative school. There you will find the issues that the community will be facing in it's not so distant future. This statement could not be any truer than it was for my community. While I was a part of this program, I dealt with a host of issues ranging from poverty, teenage pregnancy, gangs, death, the criminal justice system, and drug addiction. While there, I believed that I was making a difference in the lives of the young people in the program. However, the biggest lesson I learned quickly was that I was not going to be able to save them all. And the best example of this came in the form of a young lady who I believed had a fighting chance to change the trajectory of her life.

Prior to this young lady coming to the program, her reputation was legendary amongst the students and educators. The students whispered about how bad she was and how none of the teachers could control her. To put this into perspective, the alternative school is filled with the kids that had been kicked out of school and they were talking about how bad she was.

The day came when I received the referral for the young lady to come to the program. She had just returned from the Youth Detention Center. It was the school system's policy that any student returning from a detention facility must complete a semester at the alternative school prior to re-enrolling in the traditional setting. So, I made the appointment for the interview and she eventually arrived at the center with her grandmother. I had known her grandmother since I was a little boy. In fact, me and the grandmother's children went to grade school together. Back then, the grandmother had a reputation of being a no-nonsense parent that kept her boys in check. However, with her granddaughter, she had met her match.

I started the interview with all the pleasantries, but it quickly became evident that the young lady had intended to live up to her reputation. She put on this tough "I don't Care" attitude, but I quickly called her bluff on it. I immediately ended the interview and told the grandmother that this program would not be a good fit for her. You could see the surprise in the eyes of the grandmother as she believed that entry into the program was automatic. I knew that I was taking a chance of losing this child, but I was in a position I felt that I had to protect the rest of the students in the program as they were all on track for promotion.

The next day the phone rang, and it was the grandmother, asking for another opportunity for her granddaughter. She stated that she had a long conversation with the granddaughter, and she believed that she was ready to become a part of the program. When they returned to the center the following day in tow was an entirely different student. She was respectful, attentive, and even shared a smile or two.

The young lady started attending the program and her progress was amazing. She worked hard and never missed a day. The work she was doing was progressively getting better and better as the days passed. She was making so much progress I believed that by the time she graduated that we could have her ready for the local tech school or junior college if not more.

As I engaged the student, I learned that she had a brother that was in and out of the Youth Detention Center and that he was coming home soon. Her brother was younger than her, but it was clear that she loved him immensely. As the days neared to his arrival, she began to miss days from school. It started out with one day per week and grew to two, and three days a week. Ultimately, she started missing a week at a time. When she showed up, I would use the tough love strategy, but saw that it was not working. I transitioned to the positive behavioral support model, but that failed as well. Frustrated and at my wits end, I had concluded that it was time to remove her from the program as she had become a threat to the success of the other students.

The morning that I was going to process her paperwork to have her removed from the program, I arrived at the center early. We were having visitors from the corporate office that day. Our center had become one of the shining stars in the area and was often utilized by the sales department when other districts wanted to see the program in action. As the students came in that morning, they all collected their work materials and got busy with their work for the day. Breaking the silence of the morning activities was a knock at the door. It was the regional lead with the sales team and the potential new district representatives. They came in and greeted the staff and observed how the students were working. They chatted amongst themselves and queried the staff about the effectiveness of the program. A little while later there was another knock at the door. It was the young lady.

My heart sank when I saw her. No matter how logical the decision to sacrifice the few in order to save the many may be, it is never easy, because in the back of my mind I would always think to myself as to whether this was the best decision or not. When she came in, she retrieved her folder like normal, but on this day, she decided to stop by my desk. As she stood at my desk, she began to talk to me. I listened passively as I worked to get my desk in order. I believed that she sensed that I was not fully listening to her, so she asked to speak to me in the conference room. So, I sent her into the conference room to wait for me.

When I entered the conference room, I was fully prepared to remove her from the program, but first I believed that she needed for me to hear what she had to say. The conversation began a little slow as I felt that this was one of those moments where it was important for the student to be heard. What I did not realize was that this was going to be one of the most difficult conversations of my life.

This young lady told me how her mother had been strung out on drugs for years and had been prostituting her for money since she was ten years old to drug dealers and addicts. The more she told her story the more she began to rock back and forth in her chair. The more she rocked the more my heart shattered. It seemed that with every word she peeled back another layer of abuse. She continued to tell me that the reason that she and her brother were living with her grandmother was because of all the issues that they were having with their mother and her addiction.

While living with her grandmother, her adult uncle began to have sex with one of her middle school friends. Her friend eventually became pregnant. Then like a snake in the grass, when the friend turned up pregnant, he began to prey on his own niece, his brother's child.

As a measure of self-preservation, the young lady would act out in school and in the community whenever the sexual abuse would start as she felt safer in the youth detention center than she did at home. Going to the youth detention center was only a temporary fix to a much deeper and continuously evolving problem. She had been impregnated by her uncle. When she could no longer hide her pregnancy, she told her family her secret without revealing to them who the father was.

The uncle eventually found out that she was pregnant and instead of being afraid that she would reveal his secret he began to degrade and verbally abuse her. He called her all types of whores and told her that she was never going to do anything with her life. He damned her future by telling her that she was going to be just like her mom. Under all this distress she eventually lost the baby and after a period of healing the abuse resumed and had continued since she had returned home from the youth detention center.

By this time in the story, the young lady had begun to weep. My blood boiled as I knew the uncle, but I knew that it was important for me to maintain my composure. She began to repeat the words, "I need my grandma" repeatedly. I rushed to the phone and told the grandmother to come to the school as fast as she could.

When she arrived, I rushed her into the conference room and had to listen to this young lady tell her grandmother that her uncle, the man that the grandmother gave birth to, had been molesting her. I can't begin to put into words the pain and anguish that was in the moans from these two souls as they sat on the floor and embraced each other. The only thing that I can tell you is that the sounds traveling from the depths of their souls ran shivers through my body.

I instructed the staff to call the Department of Family and Children Services and shortly thereafter they arrived with law enforcement and whisked the grandmother and the child away. As I watched them exit the building it seemed as if time was standing still and I was trapped in a moment that was going to be with me for the rest of my life. It was also in this moment that I was awakened to the horrors of what a young person could go through without an engaged support system and the belief that no one cares for them.

In the next few years of working with the young people in this program I was able to experience a range of emotions much like a rollercoaster. There were those days when I walked in the program and felt like there was nothing that we were not going to be able to do to help those kids. Then there were those days that I wondered if I was going to be able to do enough. However, with all the training that one can receive in this line of work, nothing prepares you for when you are faced with the actual events.

There are also those stories that lift you higher than you can imagine and drop you lower than you have ever been. A young man by the name of Kevion was one of these cases. Kevion is a young man that was a part of the program that I will carry in my heart until the day I leave this earth. He was a great kid. As to how he ended up in the program I am not sure, but what I can say is that it was an environment that he was able to thrive in academically.

He would come in everyday and grab his daily assignments and get to work. When it came time for him to leave, he would make sure to throw me the peace sign before he walked out the door. Kevion did so well in the program that he became eligible to go back to the traditional school setting at the end of the semester. He and I were both so proud when we heard this news as he was going to graduate in May of that year.

After Kevion left, I would see him periodically in the community in Wal-Mart or in a local restaurant. We would exchange pleasantries and be on our way. Well, on one of the occasions that I saw him, he began to inquire about coming back to the program. At first, I was a little thrown off as I thought that being in the traditional setting was something that he wanted. Besides, he had worked so hard to accomplish his goal. However, what he shared with me was that he was able to perform better academically in my program and did not want to jeopardize his chances at graduation. I told him to speak to his counselors about it and see if there was anything that could be done to get him back into the program.

I eventually received the news that he was going to be able to come back to the program. I gave him a call to let him know that he was going to be able to return. As I shared the news with the staff, they were excited to know that he was returning as he was a kid that they loved to work with.

The day he returned to the program is one that I will never forget. It was the day before the Christmas break. The staff had gotten the students some treats and had movies for them. Kevion came in with his normal joyful self and grabbed his work for the day and got started. I was busily working interviews for new students and their parents. I felt the program had hit its groove and we were moving along quite well. While I was conducting interviews, the time had come for Kevion to leave. I looked up from the conference room and saw him at the door. He threw up the peace sign at me and walked out the door.

As I finished up with my last interview, I went to my desk to begin the second part of my day. The phone rang and it was my liaison for the county on the phone. In a very solemn tone, she asked me what I thought about Kevion. I told her that I was happy he was back and felt that him being there was going to be a good thing. Then there was a short silence and she said the words that I will never forget. "You don't know do you". When I heard these words, my heart sank.

Karen, the county liaison, went on to tell me that Kevion had been in a very bad ATV accident and was killed. As she spoke those words I glanced at the clock and said that this can't be true because he just left not even an hour ago. She reassured me that it was true. Until this day, I am unsure how that conversation ended. All I recall from that moment was sitting at my desk and watching the smiles on the staff and kids' faces as they were enjoying the festivities for the day.

I got up from my desk and very quietly called the staff into the conference room. As they came in, they sensed that something was not right. I do not believe that there are any right words to tell educators that one of their success stories lives has been lost. So, as I uttered the words to inform them that Kevion had been involved in an ATV accident and had lost his life, the tears began to roll down their cheeks. They whimpered quietly as they fought back the pain of losing this dear soul. Then as I turned to look into the classroom, it seemed that every students' eyes were gazing into the conference room. They could see the devastation on the faces of the staff.

Giving the teachers a moment, I walked out into the classroom. Justin, the de facto leader of the bunch, sighed loudly, and said, "Go ahead and tell us. We know it's something bad." So, I began to share with the group the news of Kevion's death. Silence settled in over the class as they sat there in disbelief that one of them, whom they had just seen, was suddenly taken away. I tried to be strong for the students and the staff, but inside I was torn apart.

Kevion's funeral was held in a local high school auditorium that was filled with his family and friends. When it was time to walk down the aisle to view the body, I looked into the faces of his family members and friends as they wailed in pain to the sudden loss of their loved one. As I made my way past one of his best friends, who was also in the program, I watched him as he cried uncontrollably in his mother's arms. It seemed like his heart had been ripped out of his chest as he cried in disbelief. In the past, I would have known what to say in a school setting where self-improvement was the goal, but I had no words that could begin to soothe the pain of losing a best friend at such a young age. However, what did occur to me was that there was something unnatural about burying a buddy while you are still in high school.

CHAPTER VI - ANSWERING THE CALL

If you had asked me prior to 2008 as to whether or not I would run for any elected office my immediate answer would have been no. I would have told you all of the cliché jive about how they are all corrupt and how the system does not work. I, like many Americans, simply did not believe in the election process and felt that it only benefited the few. Meanwhile, the masses of people struggle to receive the necessary resources to sustain a high quality of life. However, after working with the kids in the alternative schools and doing some work in the community, it became abundantly clear that someone had to do something more for them and the greater community. So, I began to research the issues and it became clear that the biggest barrier to reaching solutions for the problems that the students and community were facing all revolved around the lack of resources.

Whenever the conversation around resources comes up, I try to make it abundantly clear that the term "resources" is code for money. At night when we turn on our local news programs or even the national ones, we hear them talking about resources and the lack thereof. All these conversations use a non-intentional, or even intentional, language to discuss the fact that money is the real topic of conversation. What I have learned about any governmental entity or organization is that it has the money to do whatever its political will is. Therefore, the real conversation is not about the lack of resources, but if those in charge of allocating them have the desire or political will to put the necessary resources in the places where those that they represent need them.

Tired of feeling like I was spinning my wheels with volunteerism, I finally began to think about solutions to the issues that the young people and our community were facing. Fortunately, when I was working for an organization that had a strong lobbyist element to it, I was getting a lot of firsthand information as it relates to public policy and education. Additionally, working with the students and in the community helped me to see firsthand how both good and bad policy played out at the local level. So, in 2008, I made the decision to run for State Representative.

I wish I could tell you that this was a romantic venture that ended in glory, but it did not. What it did do was open my eyes a small bit as it relates to how Georgia politics work. Me, being naïve and optimistic, came home one day and told my wife that I was going to run for State Representative. When I told her that I was going to run she did not waiver and immediately said ok.

The day eventually came for qualification, so on the last day of qualifying I drove up to Atlanta to do so. When I arrived at my destination, I walked up the stairs to the State Capital and it quickly dawned on me that I had never stepped foot into this building. I admit that as intimidating as the moment was, it was also very exciting. When I opened the doors, the building was humming with its busyness. Staffers, reporters, candidates, and incumbents were hustling as the qualifying show was afoot.

I got in line and waited my turn as candidate after candidate qualified to throw their hats into the ring of chance. Finally, it was my turn. As I finished the paperwork the young man looked at me and told me that the qualifying fee was $400. Showing my greenness, I told him that I wanted to use the pauper's affidavit. The young man looked at me and asked me for my signatures. My response, "what signatures?".

This is when he told me that before I could qualify for the pauper's affidavit I had to go and get a certain percentage of the voters in the district to sign a petition showing that they supported my candidacy. Feeling about the size of an ant, I walked away with my hopes dampened. I did not have the signatures, nor did I have the money. As a matter of fact, I made that journey with just enough money to put gas in the car for the return trip to Statesboro and a combo meal from McDonald's.

So, seeing that I was not going to be able to qualify I began to make my way out of the building. As fate would have it, on my way out of the building, a gentleman that I had never met overheard my conversation with the registrar and began to talk with me as I made my way to the exit. It was an easy-going conversation and all the normal questions were asked. As we talked, he asked me why did I want to run? I told him that I was the Director of an alternative school and was tired of seeing the students struggle because of the lack of resources to serve their needs. I shared with him a few of my bright ideas about how I believed that schools should be used as community learning centers so that they could provide opportunities to the entire community and build a workforce that would attract higher paying jobs.

Our pleasantries continued as we made our way through the crowd and corridors of the capitol building. As we reached the steps on the outside of the building he reached into his pocket and pulled out his checkbook. As he looked me squarely in the eyes he said, "McCollar, I believe in you. I don't think you can win, but I believe you have a future in Georgia politics". He wrote the check out, shook my hand, wished me good luck, and went on his way. I stood there speechless. Until this day, I can't tell you who that man was, but what he ignited was a journey that I am still on until this day.

I rushed back into the building and got back in line with all my paperwork in tow. I waited patiently until it was my turn to go. I attached my signature to the remaining forms, turned in the check and became a candidate for the Georgia Assembly.

As I drove back to Statesboro, I was filled with excitement. I felt that this was a moment in my life that I was about to be able to help a lot of people and change the lives of the young people that I served. I called my wife to let her know the news. Chills ran through my body as her excitement reached through the phone and my heart pounded.

If there was ever a candidate that had no idea as to what they were doing, it was me. I knew nothing about campaigning and had never worked on a political campaign in my life. The only thing that I had on my side was the fact that I am competitive and will work hard. The other thing that I had on my side was the belief that most people have more in common than not. The only problem with these attributes is that they do not pay for campaigns.

Knowing that I needed to get campaign signs, I threw what has now become a signature campaign fundraiser for the People Over Politics movement, the BBQ plate sale. For about two weeks we worked to sell tickets for the event. When the day arrived, it seemed like people from everywhere came by to show their support. We had other candidates stopping to lend their support and shake a few hands along with local ministers and the sort showing lots of support. By the end of the event we managed to raise a whopping $700. I was so proud. I knew that we were well on our way after accomplishing this great feat.

I took the proceeds from the event and ordered 100 campaign signs. 100!!! In about a week's time the UPS truck pulled up to the door and dropped them off. As I opened the box I remember smiling from ear to ear and thinking to myself that there was no way that my opponent had these many signs and I couldn't wait until I could put them all out over a four county area. That's right, I had 100 signs to cover a four-county area. I can't help but chuckle even now as I write this.

By this time, I had come up with the political strategy to attack the largest county in the district, which was also the home county of the incumbent, During the process of campaigning I ran into Al Houston. Al was a lifelong resident of Emmanuel county and had been active in the community for many years. He was able to introduce me to some key people in the community, help put out a few signs, and get me a few speaking engagements with local civic organizations.

The one thing that I can say about Al is that he is very loyal to his beliefs, no matter what the odds may be. This became evident as he and I were able to have long discussions as we rode through the counties putting out signs. It was on these rides that he told me about all the work he had been doing in the community and how difficult it had been to move his community forward. However, not once during his conversations did, he ever let on that he had lost any hope for the future of his beloved hometown.

One day, while out putting up signs, Al and I noticed that there was a pickup truck putting out sign after sign. As we got closer, we could see that the signs were that of my opponent. It seemed that on this one stretch of highway he had more signs than there were trees. Then, to snatch any hope that I had of pulling the upset, we could see that the truck bed was filled with boxes of signs. Realizing that I was not going to be able to match him sign for sign, I decided to double down on my door knocking efforts. As a result, Al helped me to organize a canvassing campaign in Emanuel County.

In the days leading up to the canvassing event, Al had introduced me to Sister Trice. Sister Trice was a frail elderly woman. When I had met her, she was sitting in her pickup truck with a slight smile on her face telling me about the change that was needed in her community. We talked for several minutes before she had to go to her next meeting. As she pulled off, I didn't think too much about the interaction other than this was a person that was going to be a great addition to the team for Emmanuel County.

When the day arrived for the canvassing event the turnout was nowhere near that of what we had hoped for. As a matter of fact, the team consisted of Al, my eight-month pregnant wife, and myself. Nonetheless, I was determined to make a dent into this county because I knew that if I could not get any headway here then my hopes of winning the race was doomed. As the three of us discussed strategy, the front door of the church creaked open and a small head peeped in from behind the door. It was Sister Trice. I smiled as I saw her face and I felt a little relieved as this was going to be another person that could work with my wife on the phone banking while me and Al hit the doors.

We all greeted Sister Trice and began to fall into some small talk as we were preparing for the day. As we talked, I noticed that Sister Trice sat in one of the pews and began to put on her sneakers. Surprised to see this, I asked Sister Trice what was she doing? She simply replied, "I'm going with you". Her simple response spoke clearly to me that this was a woman of great will. And it also taught me not to ever judge a book by its cover when it comes to a person's desire and commitment to bring about change in their community.

As we went out into the community, Sister Trice and I began to talk. As we talked, she began to tell me more about herself. It was through this conversation that she began to tell me about her lifelong commitment to social justice and the fight to move our nation forward.

It turns out that Sister Trice was a walking piece of history. As a college student in Greensboro she was a part of the fight to integrate the lunch counters in the city. She shared with me how afraid she was during this time and even spoke about how she feared for her life. When I asked her, what gave her the power to continue to move forward she quickly replied that she did not know but felt that it was simply something that she had to do. What I know now that I didn't know back then was that I was just at the beginning of what was going to be a long journey in the fight to move my part of the world forward. Sister Trice was now clearly in her seventies and was continuing the good fight to leave this world a little better than when she found it and this fact was evident as she spent the next several hours knocking on doors with Al and I encouraging people to go to the polls.

During the time of me running my campaign to be a state representative, there was a huge presidential race that was a foot on the national level. 2008 was a year where there were no incumbents and there were plenty of candidates from both the republican and democratic parties. Early in that election cycle, I liked the young Senator from North Carolina, John Edwards.

For me, John came across very Kennedy-ish and was clearly very smart. But more than that, I liked his stance on poverty. I, like him, believe that poverty is one of the greatest issues that our nation is facing. So, when he went to a poor section of New Orleans to launch his campaign, I was very impressed. To me this was a candidate that was too good to be true. And in hindsight, he was.

There was another promising candidate that was in the race for the presidency of the United States as well, Barack Obama. He too was a young senator that was from the state of Illinois. At first glance, I believed him to be extremely intelligent, charismatic and one of the greatest orators that I had ever heard. However, I was unsure of his policies, but I still liked him because I believed he had what it was going to take to get him a long way in the world of politics.

As time progressed, Barack Obama became a candidate that inspired a new generation of people to get engaged in the political process. His team was filled with young people from all walks of life. They were Black, White, Gay, Straight, Lesbian, Hispanic, and more. They were energized. But more than that, they were optimistic about the future of our nation.

Barack's message of hope and change came at a very pivotal time in our nation's history. The nation was tired from the labor of constant war. The housing market was in shambles and the economy was in the tank. At this point America was losing hundreds of thousands of jobs a month and it seemed that there was not going to be an end to any of this any time soon. However, his message was so powerful that it fueled the flame of a countless number of individuals to join his campaign.

One of these individuals was a young lady by the name of Naomi. Naomi was a young college student at Georgia State University in Atlanta. She was so moved by the Obama campaign that she decided to take a semester off from college so she could dedicate herself to the campaign. In doing so, she was ultimately hired by the Obama campaign and then assigned to the region that included Statesboro.

As fate would have it, she and I had met at a Democratic Party meeting. There, I found out that she was staying with some friends and sleeping in a spare room sacrificing all the familiar comforts of home. This was impressive to me. Another thing that truly impressed me about Naomi was that she was a ball of this non-stop positive energy. It was so clear that she was truly dedicated to the Obama campaign and its message of hope and change. Admittedly, by this time he was winning me over as well. However, there was still some work to be done to get me there fully.

To cover more ground for both the Obama Campaign and mine, she and I teamed up to register people to vote and canvass our region. We would work late into the evenings roaming the streets in the local neighborhoods encouraging people to be a part of the change. It was on one night that I realized the power of an inspired people. Late one evening, Naomi and I were out canvassing and registering people to vote in Morris Heights Apartments in Statesboro. Night had fallen and I was out talking to a group of my students and their parents about the issues. As I stood and talked to the large group that had assembled, I watched Naomi go from door to door working to register people to vote. After she had knocked on every door in the complex, she stopped people as they were returning home as they were getting out of their cars. It was at this moment that I realized that if a young white female could come to my hometown and work tirelessly in predominantly black and poor neighborhoods to move our people to the polls then I could do more.

While she was here, we registered hundreds of people to vote. However, when the Obama campaign realized that Georgia was no longer in play, they quickly shifted their resources to the areas of the country that they believed would be most beneficial. This meant that it was time for Naomi to leave. Though I was saddened to see her go, I understood that the goal was to get Barack Obama elected as the next president of the United States.

As for my campaign, we continued the work, but the task seemed more daunting with each passing day. The more I campaigned, the more I saw the good that my opponent was doing for his community. He had secured funding for the local tech school and community college that allowed them to grow and provide additional services to the community. He also secured funding for infrastructure projects and aided many local business owners on their journey to success. All politics aside, this man was doing a good job. I just believed that I would do more.

On the evening prior to election day, I drove to all of the precincts in the district so I could put my signs out front so that the people would have one last chance to see my name prior to going in to cast their ballots. As I was doing this, a lot of thoughts raced through my mind. My heart sped up every time I thought about winning the race. My stomach sank when I thought about losing. Until this day, there has been no change about election eve. It is always nerve racking, because I am constantly questioning myself as to whether I've done everything possible to come out successfully on the other side.

Election Day was finally here. It seemed so surreal for me. The day that I had been working towards for the past several months was finally here. The wife and I ate breakfast at home and got the kids ready so we could go vote. When we got to the polls it was amazing. It seemed like people were coming from everywhere to vote. You could feel the electricity in the air. I would like to say that all the excitement was about my campaign, but it was not. It was about that young senator from Illinois and the possibility of him being the next president of the United States and the first African American to hold the office.

After casting our ballots, we decided to ride around to the precincts to see what the turnout was looking like. As we drove around, we laughed and joked as normal. Each precinct looked busy in our local county, so we decided to drive over to the largest county in our district, which was also the home district for the incumbent. It took us about 45 minutes to get there as we pulled up; we finally saw the person that I was running against. There, live and in the flesh, was Butch Parrish.

In the preceding months, Butch Parrish had become an enigma to me. It seemed that everywhere that I went on the campaign trail I heard his name. However, it was not until this moment that I had finally set eyes on the actual man as he stood in front of his large RV passing out hot dogs to the people as they came and went from casting their ballots.

It was in that moment that I realized that I knew very little about being a good candidate for the people. Yes. I had done all of the volunteer work in the community and had a vitae filled with good deeds and my heart was in the right place, but I did not realize that one must make a transition from community activist to being a candidate for public office. On the campaign trail, I had heard the stories about how Butch helped this person and that person. I even realized one day that the highway that I traveled from work to his home county was named after him. What Butch had done very well was to tell his story to the people and make his actions relevant and visible to them.

For years, this man had been involved with local politics. And it was through his elected offices that he was able to help a lot of people. While out one day canvassing prior to election day, I stopped by a barber shop in Butch's hometown to visit with the owner and talk with a few of his customers about supporting my campaign. They all sat there and listened to my spill about how I would like to serve in the assembly and be a voice for our young people and the community. I got the normal round of questions and was ultimately asked the question as to why they should support me over Butch? I told them of my passion for the people and my desire to do something for the everyday people of the district. Upon finishing my statement, the barber quickly told me that he would not be in business if it was not for Butch helping him. Stunned by the moment, I stood there in the immediate revelation that small town politics and politics in general are about the deliverables to the people that's going to support you. For that barber, it was not about my good will, but the opportunity that he was afforded to be able to take care of his family. In this case, being a democrat or republican did not matter. What mattered was his bottom line.

As the clock began to wind down on election night there was a fever in the air. America was on the precipice of electing its first African American President. It seemed that our beloved nation was about to turn the page and begin a new chapter. By this point, my hope was simple, maybe I would be able to ride the coattails of change into the Georgia Assembly.

When the polls closed that night, the nation had elected its first African American President. And for the first time in the nation's history a Black family would be calling the White House home. As for me, my fate was a little different. I was soundly defeated by the incumbent. Though I was disappointed in the outcome, I have always had a knack for being able to be honest with myself. And in this case, I knew I was not the best candidate for the job.

CHAPTER VII - FANNING THE FLAME

In the time following my race, there was a difference in me. Before the race, the bulk of the work I focused on involved young people. Since the race, my work began to transition to things that were more politically minded. I was convinced that political activism was the best way to turn my community around. Now, with the fire for change burning in my soul, I became more involved in the local Democratic Party. I started out by attending some meetings and eventually sitting on a few committees. The local party was made up of a few die-hard Democrats that had been loyal to the local party for quite some time and a few newbies. The membership was low, and the party had not flipped a seat of any sort in a while, but it did have representation at the congressional, county, and city levels.

As I grew in the party, I was able to learn a lot under the mentorship of people like George Jackson, Liz Johnson, John Brown, Pat Gillis and many more. It is because of them that I was able to get the wind beneath my wings and take flight in the party. Ultimately, this growth led to me becoming its chair.

Becoming chair of the party was an opportunity that I was extremely excited about. From the start the beliefs of the party were things that resonated with me. The ideas of diversity and inclusion, affordable health care, and investment into education were things that I was immensely passionate about. I also believed that if more people in our community were more aware of what the party was fighting for, then the party would be able to grow exponentially and be a voice for change within our community.

Understanding that people can't support what they don't know about led me to push to raise the profile of the organization. When I first came on board with the organization the signature fundraiser for the party was a small potluck style dinner at the local community center. The attendance for this event was sparse and typically attended by the local democratic loyalist with our Congressman, John Barrow, being the main attraction. I saw this being a huge opportunity for me to move the party in a different direction while funding a campaign war chest for the party.

After thinking about this opportunity for a while, I came up with the idea of having the Democratic Independence Gala. This event would be the signature fundraiser for the organization. It would be an opportunity for the people in the community to get dressed up and mix and mingle with the stars and rising stars of the Democratic Party from across the state while learning more about the party.

I went about the business of planning the event with the help of my wife and our good friend Shontelle. The process was easy, but the difficult part was deciding who was going to be the keynote speaker for this event. Being that it was the first event of its kind for the local party, I wanted to make sure that we had the right person. As I made inquiries about potential speakers, a host of names came up. The names that initially came up were the familiar names that spoke often at local events. Believing that we needed a fresh and new voice, I expanded my search and was eventually given the name of a young state representative that was a true rising star: Stacey Abrams.

As I reached out to Stacey's office, I was unsure of whether she would have time or even want to make the trip down to Statesboro for an upstart event. However, to my surprise, her team's immediate response was a simple response. "She will be there". At this moment I knew two things: I made the best decision by reaching out to her office. Secondly, the person that I reached out to was dedicated to something that was bigger than herself.

When the night of the Gala came the event went off flawlessly. The venue was decorated beautifully, the people looked great, and it was filled with new faces. Everyone was filled with cheer and their faces were beautifully adorned with glowing smiles. As we sat and finished our meals Stacey gave one of the most riveting speeches I had ever heard. It was like her words were speaking to all my beliefs. She spoke of boldly embracing yourself and your beliefs and how the best days of our nation are in front of us. By the time she had concluded her speech it was right with my soul to continue to move boldly within our community and fight to return the power of its governing bodies to its people.

Since this night, the gala has gone on for a decade now. The event has grown to the point that we are now just short of 200 plus attendees at each event which is a big deal for a small rural community in southeast Georgia. Additionally, since Stacey Abrams, we have had Andrew Young, Jason Carter, Francys Johnson, John Barrow, John Ossoff, Teresa Tomlinson, Stacey Evans, Nikema Williams, and many others to come and be a part of our event. This event has raised thousands of dollars for our small community's party and our numbers at the polls have grown consistently.

During planning for the Gala, I was also involved in another campaign. The County Commission seat for my district came up and I decided to make a run for it. The seat was occupied by longtime incumbent Anthony Simmons. Anthony was a good guy and his family had a long history of working within the community. As a matter of fact, his dad and uncle were stalwarts in the fight for equality in our community.

I decided to run for this office because I believed that I would bring a fresh and new voice to the county commission. I believed that this was important at the time as the community was working through the renovating process of one of its historical parks. In the state of Georgia there is the duplication of services mandate that works to save resources within our communities. So, in our community, the local parks are managed by the county commission whether they are located inside of a municipality or not. I, like many others in the community, felt that their voices were not adequately heard in this process.

A part of this process was a push to demolish a building that was one of the first African American schools in the area. It would be replaced with a new facility that could potentially be used as a community center. There the new facility could potentially provide wrap around services for an area that was struggling with poverty and activities for the youth. Though the new building was at the center of some tough debate, it was quite evident that the decision to move forward with the demolishing of the historic building and to reduce the area for basketball and tennis was a done deal.

The day finally came when it was time for the community to give feedback to the commissioners. The room was packed. It was in this meeting that I made the plea that the people in this area preferred basketball and enjoyed a longstanding basketball culture. Feeling that my statements reached deaf ears, I made the comment that every person that was up there was elected and could be voted out if they are unwilling to honor the wishes of the community that this park resided in. The commissioner that took exception to this statement was Anthony which was ironic as he was the county commissioner that I would eventually run against.

Entering this 2010 County Commission campaign, the lesson that I brought with me from my state representative campaign was that I needed to touch as many voters in the district as possible and be able to tell my story as to why I was running. So, after work, I would go into the neighborhoods and knock on the doors and talk to the people about the issues they were facing. Two main issues seemed to come up: the fact the young people did not have anything to do and there were not enough good paying jobs. When I was speaking with them, I could see the weight of these matters weighing heavily on their souls.

As I continued to campaign, the question that I began to ask myself was, "What has he done for the people in his district?" I eventually began to ask the people this very question and many of them could not answer it or stated that they did not know who he was. This was astonishing as he had been there for three or so terms by now.

Anthony came from a family that had strong roots in the community as it relates to social activism and equality. He was the nephew of the late great Donnie Simmons and the son of Bobby Simmons. Both men worked tirelessly to help move our small town forward. As a matter of fact, his uncle's legendary commitment to the people is still being talked about today. In his uncle's later years his health began to fail, but he managed to continue to work to educate the people about the importance of voting. Even as a double amputee, Donnie wheeled himself into the election's office, checked out a voting machine, and set it up in a church so he could show the people how to use it. As I write this, I shudder to think where Statesboro would be without the hard work and dedication of people like Donnie Simmons.

I will be the first to admit that at this time in my life I was still very naïve and idealistic about the political campaigning process. I still believed in the magic of being the best candidate. I still believed that great ideas and good sportsmanship were key attributes in the game of politics. Well, this was about to change because I was about to get a crash course in local politics and what it means to do battle on the local level.

Anthony knew his base of voters better than any other candidate that I have ever run into, and he did not waste any time working on people who did not vote nor whom he had to persuade to vote. This type of efficiency allowed him to spend his time where it really mattered. So, while I was out knocking on every door possible, he was spending his time in the circle of people who had a high tendency to vote. He was hitting the churches while encouraging his friends and family members to go vote.

Anthony also had an arsenal of surrogates who would campaign in the circles that he was unable to get to. One of his strongest campaign surrogates was a long-time city councilman by the name of Gary Lewis. Gary was the undefeated champion of local politics for the area. It seemed that with every election cycle, Gary had a crew of people and a rumored scandal working to get him out of office, but he would beat them all. So, with him being a champion for my opponent made things that much tougher for me as a young political start up. It also meant that the surrogates were able to say the things that Anthony could not say.

A good example of this is when his team put into the rumor mill that I was not from Statesboro. In local politics not being from where you are running for office is a cardinal sin in a small town. Though this rumor was clearly not true, it afforded Anthony the opportunity for his hands to remain clean in a sense. The power of his surrogates lies in the fact that they not only got to tell his story, but they got to tell others why they supported his campaign. And consequently, if they just so happen to say something unflattering or untrue about me then it didn't have as much of a negative effect on his campaign.

Another nuance that I learned in this race was the great Houdini disappearance act of my campaign signs. I laugh now as I write this, but this was not a joking matter for me at the time. There is no worse feeling than working a forty plus hour a week job to get off and go place signs up so that someone could either steal them or throw them into the woods. This used to burn me up! However, what I learned was this act was not personal, but strategy.

In this era in small town politics signage was powerful and predated the social media's effect on local campaigns in rural Georgia. So, for every opponent sign that was discarded it meant that fewer people would recognize the name at the ballot box. What I have learned in the years since is that this is a common practice in small town politics, but it is a practice that I have forbidden my campaigns to get involved in. Why? Because I believe that there is a significant lesson to be learned in a candidate that is willing to allow his team to stoop so low as to steal the property of their opponent. Besides, if you will steal a sign, what else will you steal or do in the name of politics?

In this race I began to build my reputation as a hard campaigner. My signs were popping up everywhere and the number of doors knocked grew every day. It was my mission to knock on as many doors as possible, and that is what I set out to do every single day.

While out knocking on doors, I went into the neighborhood where Anthony lived. I had family and friends in this neighborhood so I felt confident about the number of votes that I would be able to get out of it. What I did not know was that I was going to have the chance to meet a local legend in Alethea Lewis.

Mrs. Lewis and her husband, the late Charlie Lewis, were both political and social activists in our community. The two of them were advocates for equality and economic opportunity. They practiced what they preach by opening a business in the Black community that was a staple in it for many years. In this chance meeting, she and I had the opportunity to talk about the race and my family. Now, if you are a true Southerner, you know the importance of the conversation about what family you come from is, and you also recognize that this is an opportunity for you and the person you are talking with to connect. So, as I began to explain who my family was and how I had become familiar with the work of the Lewises we were able to create a bond that only has grown stronger as time has progressed.

As our conversation was coming to an end, Mrs. Lewis said some words to me that I carried with me until this day: she believed that I was going to win the race. To have this blessing from an elder in Statesboro meant everything to me, and it gave me the fire to continue fighting. In the following weeks, I was a man on fire. I printed more flyers and knocked on more doors. I was on the radio stations and I was at the churches. I worked diligently all the way to the finish. I worked so hard that people began to ask me why I was so passionate about this race. And I would tell them that I simply believe that I will be a better representative for the people of that district.

When the day of the election came, I was ready. I lined the street near the precinct with my signs early that morning and was back out to wave at the voters as they paraded into the precinct to vote. While out waving at the people, a dark-skinned older gentleman approached me with a bewildered look on his face. As he came closer, I recognized that this was Anthony's father. The legendary Bobby Simmons, the brother to the late great Donnie Simmons. When he got close enough to me, he asked one simple question: "Why are you doing this?" You are tearing the community apart." Standing in shock at his words, I could only reply that I believed whole-heartedly that I am the best person for the job. He walked away without ever saying another word to join his son as they greeted the voters as well.

Unknown to me at the time, there was a debate in the black political community about my candidacy. On one side were those loyal to the established politicos of the community, and on the other side were those looking for a breath of fresh air in the political world in Bulloch County. And at the crux of this argument was, why am I challenging another Black candidate?

When I signed my name on the line to become the next County Commissioner for my district, I did not think about the fact I was running against another Black person. The only thing I was focused on was the fact that I believed that I was the best person for the job and that I was willing to fight for it. What I have learned since then is that race still matters in small town politics even if both candidates as Black. For some, the belief is that it's best to stick to what we know even if it is ineffective. And for others, it's the belief that change is sometimes warranted even if it comes from within the group. In this County, for Blacks to get any form of representation a court case had to be filed where there could be districts drawn so that blacks would have a chance at viable representation politically. The candidate that I was running against was the relative of those who had fought to get this feat accomplished. In hindsight, I can see why this was such a big deal for those involved, because my actions could have been misconstrued as being disrespectful or unappreciative of the work of those who had come before me.

As election day progressed, I stood on the corner waving my heart out. I was greeted with both cheers and jeers. An educator who had taught me in school slowly rode by yelling out his window that he just voted for my opponent. When I heard these words my heart sank, because this was a teacher that I had looked up to for many years. He was a shaper in many of my beliefs, one of which was to always fight like hell no matter what the odds were.

When the polls closed and the last of the voters made their way through the lines, I began to gather my signs so I could head down to the courthouse to get the results of the race. I quickly finished the task and to the election's office. I drove into the parking lot and saw what seemed like a sea of cars. I parked and jumped out and made my way to the front door. As I walked in the facility, I could see all the movers and shakers of the local political scene. In the mix as well were the reporters from the local paper and area T.V. stations. There was a special fervor in the air that you can only get on an election night as everyone there was awaiting the results of some hard-fought races.

I can't lie and say that I was cool as a cucumber because my heart was racing. Up until this point, the thought of me losing had never entered my mind. I believed that I had done everything possible to come out victorious in the race. I had knocked on all the doors, put up all the signs, and hit the radio stations with tenacity. However, to my disappointment, I didn't do enough to win the race. Anthony had beaten me by a little more than one hundred and twenty votes. In his remarks to the newspaper, Anthony praised me for my tenacity and said he believed that one day I was going to do some big things in the world of politics in Bulloch County. In his kind words, he showed me that humility is essential to being a great public servant.

As I drove home that night, the faces of the people who worked on the campaign continuously rolled through my mind. These people were far from rich, but they believed in the campaign, its mission, and its vision. Along with these thoughts was this overwhelming sense of guilt that I had let them down. I also reflected the faces of the people that I encountered as I went door to door and told them that I would fight for them, their children, and their families. I can't put into words the inner conflict that I had that night, but I am sure that this was the moment the words People Over Politics transitioned from being a three-word slogan to a movement that was raging inside of me.

CHAPTER VIII - IT'S CHESS

Following the 2010 race, I began to focus on self-improvement while continuing to work in the community. I was fortunate enough to become a part of an organization whose mission was economic development and youth development. There I was able to connect the dots between advocating at the representative level and the work at the grassroots level.

The organization was Goodwill Industries. Often when individuals think about Goodwill it is typically regarding the thrift stores that we see in many shopping plazas across the country. Well, there is a whole lot more to the organization than what many of us see. It is an organization that works with people with disabilities, young people, and communities in areas ranging from economic development to youth development depending on the needs of the people.

The time at Goodwill was a period of tremendous personal growth. I was able to learn so much from the organization and the people that I encountered while working there. And when I say this, I am mainly talking about the people that the organization served and the community partners that worked at the grassroots level providing essential services.

One of the first things that I witnessed there was the power of how gainful employment improved the self-esteem of those that had disabilities who were overlooked by employers. For them, working for Goodwill gave them purpose, joy, and a family away from home. I recall walking through the building in route to the back of a warehouse where my office was housed and hearing the good mornings as I strolled through. I would say my good morning in return and looked on as they took so much pride in their work. These mornings were good moments for me. However, they were not the reason for being there. I was hired at Goodwill to work with youth in at-risk situations for a program that had just received federal funding to provide mentoring services. I was tasked to start this program from scratch. This was a challenge that I embraced wholeheartedly.

I set out to build a team that was passionate about young people and smart. The first person that I hired was a young man by the name of Jermaine Durham. He and I had worked together at Educational Service of America where I was able to witness firsthand his dedication to young people and his desire to share knowledge. The two of us became the driving force in the office. We were aggressive and determined to save the life of every child we encountered. We knocked on doors, attended community meetings, worked with the school system, youth organizations and the like. We recruited youth and youth mentors. We cut our teeth as advocates in the community and on Capitol Hill. However, during it all, that recurring feeling of there needs to be more done to change the conditions of the young people continued to eat away at me. I still believed that I could do more to exact real change by creating policy that would change the behavior of governing bodies.

The chance to scratch this itch came about with an opportunity to run for office in the city of Statesboro. In 2012 a longtime City Council member, Mr. Tommy Blitch, decided to resign from the council due to health issues. As chance would have it, he was also my City Councilman. I decided to run for the seat as I believed that I would be a good councilman and would represent the people of that district well. But more so, I would work to bring about real change within the city. So, when the time came for me to qualify to run for office, I was there front and center.

This was the race where it became clear that I had caught the attention of some local politicians who had opposing ideas as to what the future of our city should look like. To me, this was a race that I could see a clear path to victory and a way to begin to write a new chapter in our city's history. It was in a district that was a majority minority, extremely progressive, and I was well known in it. What I quickly learned about politics was that this is truly a game of chess and not checkers.

When qualifying for office was completed, four candidates had put their names in the hat to become the next city councilman for my district. Two conservatives with great name recognition were among those entering the race. One of them was a local hotel and restaurant owner. The family and I often visited his restaurant and shared some great memories of us acting silly and telling jokes. The second was a talk show host for a local radio station. On the more progressive side, it was me and another young man that was African American as well.

This was a special election being held at the same time as the presidential election. For the second time, I was on the ballot with President Obama, and this fact was not missed by those who opposed my candidacy. From the beginning, the idea of sitting elected officials and a few special interests was to put a second African American into the race so that the Black vote would be split. Their hope for the race would go into a runoff was a key part of their strategy to win. Their belief was that African Americans were not going to come back out for a runoff election for a city council seat. This race would seem unimportant to them when compared to the other races that were on the ballot that November. Especially on a ballot that had Barack Obama on it in his re-election bid.

All four candidates dived into the race by hitting the doors in the district and making their case as to why they would be the best representative for District One. However, amid this personal advocacy, the political tricks of old began to raise their ugly head. The business owning candidate hired a gentleman that we refer to, affectionately of course, as "Uncle Ruckus" to be a part of his team. "Uncle Ruckus" is a local self-proclaimed Black political genius. He is a character that is never seen until it is election time and when he is seen it is typically in a bad light. His political genius is embedded in him destroying the signs of the opponent, bad mouthing the opponent, and selling himself to the old guard he is the man that can garner them the black vote and certain victory. In the years that I have known Uncle Ruckus what I have noticed is that whenever he is working for a candidate then that candidate loses. Nonetheless, in this race he became more of a headache than a factor.

My campaign, like any other, runs on having the money to get the resources that are needed to win. Uncle Ruckus understands this. So, he will go out and steal or destroy the signage of his foes and this was not missed on our campaign. It was our luck that he lived in the district that I was campaigning in. So, on his route to sell his pictures in a local shopping center, which was one of his many side hustles, he would pick up each of my campaign's signs along the way and replace them with the signs of his candidate. There are no words to explain how much this burned me up as we were a campaign that had little to no money and was fueled by dedicated volunteers with little financial resources themselves.

The sign theft had gotten so bad that I eventually had to reach out to the business candidate and tell him what was going on. As I spoke to him, he stated that he didn't believe that Uncle Ruckus would steal the signs, but he would speak to him about it. So, as I walked away from the conversation, I gave the candidate the benefit of the doubt and hoped that things would get better. They did not. The signs kept disappearing, but we compensated this act by focusing on touching the people in the district by doubling down on our canvassing efforts.

As time progressed, word had reached us that many believed that I had become one of two front runners for the race and favorite to win. However, the question was, were we going to be able to get enough people to the polls to avert the runoff? The hopes for accomplishing this goal was high, but we knew that it was a lofty goal. The vote was split four ways and in the state of Georgia it is the candidate with fifty percent plus one vote that wins the race, not a simple majority.

As election day rolled around, we were excited and believed that we were going to be close to a victory. It seemed that all the conditions were right, and we believed that we had put in the necessary work to win. So, as the numbers began to come in, we immediately knew that the race was going into a runoff. In fact, we were not even the top vote getter in the race. We ran second to a candidate who was a local radio personality and a strong conservative in a district that was overwhelmingly progressive. His strategy was good as he focused on the conservative voters that were most likely to go to the polls, laced with a little fear mongering about other candidates while deflecting from his own questionable attributes.

That night President Obama won re-election and we celebrated as we began to have our initial conversation regarding the runoff election. I felt pretty good about our chances in the race as the district was a predominantly progressive district, and we had worked it pretty good during the general election cycle. As we worked the doors during the general election the people were extremely excited about going to the polls, so we thought that this energy would carry over to the runoff election. It did not.

The turnout for the runoff election was not what we needed. The excitement we saw in the general election was gone. The hope of being able to ride the Obama wave was gone as we lost the race by a little more than one hundred votes. The lesson that I learned was that it is not smart to hitch your wagon to another campaign with hopes of winning. Riding a bigger candidate's coattails is good, but you must make sure that your campaign is making enough headway so that you can have some energy of your own.

Following the 2012 race for city council, I was not low like I was following my previous races as I felt that I had learned enough of the technicalities of politics to win any other race that I would be involved in. So, as the new year rolled in, I began to focus on the small rental company my family had started and continued to be active in the community. I was selected to be the keynote speaker for the local MLK celebration and received a local award for being the civic person of the year. As I began to find some normalcy in my life, in the back of my mind the death of a young kid in Florida continued to resurface in my thoughts.

CHAPTER IX - A JUSTIFIED UNREST

In February of 2012, Trayvon Martin was shot and killed in Sanford, Florida by George Zimmerman. The trial for this case began in the summer of 2013. As I monitored this case, I became emotionally attached to it as not only could I have been Trayvon Martin at that age, but he could have very well been one of my sons. I, like most of America, saw the photos of young Trayvon Martin run across our social media feed. However, what broke my heart the most was the audio recording of the event.

As chance would have it, a resident of Trayvon's father's complex heard someone yelling for help and called 911. While the resident was on the phone with the emergency operator, what is believed to be Trayvon's voice could be heard in the background screaming for help. Then suddenly, BANG!!! The sound of a gun goes off and the yelling immediately STOPS!!! These few seconds must have been the most heart wrenching moments imaginable for the parents of this young man. I can't imagine the horror and heartbreak of hearing the last cries for help from their child.

The death of Trayvon Martin sent a shockwave through our country and awakened a new generation of young people, which gave birth to the #BLACKLIVESMATTER movement. For the older generations, the passion in these young people was exciting and frightening at the same time. The movement organized millions across the nation via social media and spurred protests across the country in cities both large and small. The city of Statesboro was no exception. Students on the campus of Georgia Southern University and throughout the community organized and marched to the courthouse lawn where they expressed their anger about the death of Trayvon Martin and their dismay with the system. During the protest there was both hope and frustration. On one hand, the young people were enraged by the death of a young man, but then there was hope because it was clear that the fight for social justice and equality would not be missed on this generation.

I was invited to speak to the crowd of young people at the protest. As I took the microphone and looked into the faces of the crowd, I could see the pain, anger, and disbelief in their eyes. As they stood there, in a light drizzle, I could see tears stream down the faces of some of the young ladies as they did all they could to present themselves as being the new shoulders of strength for generations to come. In times like this, I can't help but notice the sorrowful beauty of humanity standing in the gap of pain for those in need and presenting themselves as the bridge of progress for our nation.

As I began to speak, I looked throughout the crowd and saw the many hues and colors that made up our community. I could see that we had pastors and civic leaders. I could see that we had the old and the young alike. And then my eyes rested upon Ms. Glennaria Martin, a member of the local board of education and the only elected official in the crowd. Shockingly, I did not grow angry, I simply settled into the understanding that this was the period that we all have been waiting for. This was the moment that our community and nation was preparing to go in a drastically different direction. This was that moment that I realized that an entire generation had answered the call to chart the path of a nation.

The death of Trayvon Martin had little to do with politics, but more with the inability of our nation to heal from its original sin. It also spoke to the soul of our nation. It was a simple question of what is right and what is wrong. And for the justice system to find George Zimmerman innocent was once again another miscarriage of justice by a system that has lacked the moral fortitude to address the ills of its institutions. However, for too many other people, the issue was not about right and wrong. It was about something else, and that was maintaining the status quo. And this fact was not missed on our community.

Statesboro, like many other cities across the nation, had taken silence as consent for many issues. For decades, the people of our nation have seen atrocious acts carried out and deafening silence filled the spaces where the voices of concern or dissent were supposed to be. And as time progressed, that deafening silence became the expectation. So, when that space becomes filled with the true concern that had always been there, it disrupts the status quo, and this sends shockwaves through the community. As a part of my message on that evening, I encouraged the young people not to remain silent in the face of injustice, but to lift their voices and let their truth ring proud and free. It was their moment, our moment, to let the world know that we have the courage to speak truth boldly.

As I drove home that night, I knew that the people of our community and this generation longed for the very thing that I longed for as a citizen: To have leadership that focuses on the needs of people. And for me, this meant more than just paving some roads and passing some laws just for the sake of being able to say you did something when election times rolled around. I, like the people, longed for leadership that was going to find solutions to tough problems and be honest with them no matter what. And I, for one, wanted to have leadership that could look at a social ill and have the moral fortitude to say truthfully what is wrong and what is right. I knew then that the words of the great leader Dean C.W Grant are true: "If it is to be, it is up to me." We are truly the heroes that we have been waiting for.

CHAPTER X - A STEP TOWARDS DESTINY

The following fall of 2013 was election time for the city of Statesboro, and I had decided that I would run to be its next Mayor. This race, unlike those before, was very different. I believed that I had been prepared for a successful campaign and had the policy ideas such as updating the city's infrastructure, promoting inclusive excellence, economic development, youth development, and neighborhood revitalization that could move the city forward. Prior to my qualifying, three other candidates qualified: the incumbent Joe Brannen, Jan Moore, and Bill Thomas. When I entered the race, I felt that I had pretty good name recognition considering that I had run for City Council the year before. However, what I missed was that my run for city council was my first introduction to mainstream Statesboro.

Since the age of fourteen I had been working as a community volunteer and organizer in Statesboro. In the mid 1980's, I worked diligently with local legends like Loretta Williams and Lonnie Simmons to shed light on the AIDS and crack epidemics. In high school I stayed active with these organizations and eventually became president of the Afro-American Club in my senior year. This was a 200-member organization that had a heavy community presence. The organization was the largest in its history with a membership roll made up of students from across the spectrum.

Additionally, While I was away at college, I continued to return home and work on different projects and speak at different events. So, when I returned to Statesboro, it was no surprise to those who knew me that I picked up right where I left off before leaving. Because of this, I assumed that I knew most people in the city and that most people knew me. However, this was clearly not the case.

When I announced my run for mayor it became obvious that the city of Statesboro was a community of two tales. In one tale, it was a traditional southern city with old families who pulled the strings of all the major happenings in the city. In fact, a small group of men that were a part of this circle boasted that the city had not had a mayor that did not have their approval. In the second tale of the city, Statesboro was a bustling southern jewel with a diverse population and a lot of progressive thinkers. A city where people believed that its best days are in front of it. And it was a city where the people also believed that if they worked together, then anything was possible. Also, in this tale, the city had a past where it had not been the most inclusive place. However, those that were more progressive want to rid the city of this stigma and embrace a future where all its citizens and visitors felt welcomed. Understanding the significance of both tales, I started my journey to become the next mayor of the city of Statesboro.

The campaign for mayor was my fourth attempt at elected office. So, when I started to campaign, I was met, quite often, with the "oh, he is running for something else" expression. Candidly speaking, I was not surprised or put off by this reaction because I knew that these were the same people who were going to support our movement because we all agreed that there had to be some change in our city.

From day one, nobody mistook our campaign for being one with tons of funding. We were a group of people who simply believed that we could make a change in our community, and that is what fueled us. As a matter of fact, we managed to scrape up enough funds for handbills and signs, and that was pretty much it. And at the time, we were thankful to raise those funds as we understood that the people, we were fighting for often did not have the disposable income to donate large sums of money to political campaigns. As a matter of fact, many change agents face this issue when they enter the political arena and it did not miss us.

The lack of funding became a barrier that prevented us from being able to get our message out to the masses in an efficient manner. We had to focus a lot of our attention on our ground game by going out and knocking on doors. Though this method is labor intensive, I believe it is the best way to build relationships with the people that you want to represent and to hear from them first-hand about their concerns.

As time progressed our support began to swell. We started to pick up momentum and a small buzz around our campaign. One day I visited an elderly woman who lived in a small apartment on the north side of the city. When I knocked, she answered the door with a smile and was dressed in her finest church clothes. As I began to introduce myself, she interrupted me by saying that she already knew who I was. She went on to tell me that she had been paying attention to the work that we had been doing and that each time she saw us it was like God was walking with us. I stood there speechless. she went on to say a few more encouraging words then hugged me and sent me on my way. The feeling that I had walking away from this encounter cannot be put into words but suffice it to say that I was deeply moved by the spirit of this gentle soul. I have yet to see her again and often wondered about her. I have knocked on that door a time or two since then, but there has been no answer.

As the campaign progressed, our hard work began to pay off as we became one of the two front runners in the race. The four candidates were a mixed bag that really told the story of a city at a crossroads. The incumbent represented the traditional mainstream interests of the city; a business owner that was deeply involved with the happenings of the city government; and a local educator who was a contributor to the local newspaper, and me.

The educator and I began to pull away from the group. On the surface of things, it appeared that she was leaps and bounds ahead, but we believed that our knocking on doors was going to pay off. We understood that signs did not vote, but people did. We were making more of a genuine connection to the voters of the city. However, the barrier we were running into was that of disbelief in the possibility of our city having an African American Mayor.

Prior to my candidacy, only one African American had run for Mayor of the City of Statesboro and that was Rev. Donald Logan in the early 1990's. Since his race, Statesboro did not have another contested mayoral election until the 2013 race. So, the mere fact that the city was seeing its first mayoral race in more than two decades was a novelty. The idea that this race could possibly be the one where the glass ceiling for women and African Americans could be broken added a lot more intrigue to it.

Statesboro's African American community had been nearly totally left out of the greater political process. This community, like many others across the country, had its assigned seats at the table. There were special districts drawn to ensure that there was minority representation at the table, but never enough to be able to make real change. For the county commission there are two seats out of six that are designated for minority representation as well as on the board of education and the city council of Statesboro. Respectively, the two seats on the board of education and county commissioners reflected this diversity where at this time there was only one African American on the council for the city of Statesboro. The second seat for the city was occupied by the opposite of what that district's population represented.

As a result of the lack of diverse representation, the voices and needs of the African American community went unheard and when raised seemed to be disruptive to the status quo.

Consequently, many in the African American community grew frustrated and apathetic to local politics and failed to participate. So, it was no surprise that for many in this election that my mere candidacy was seen as divisive as I was now encouraging those that had been systematically disenfranchised from the process to now come out and let their voices be heard. I wholeheartedly believed that this was the time for things in our community to be disrupted as we were suffering from some greater problems that I simply did not believe those in the current leadership roles understood nor could effectively address.

When I began this race, I ran with the belief that I was the best candidate. I believed that via my community activism, education, and professional experience I was uniquely prepared to better represent the entirety of the city's populous and address the issues that the city was facing. And this was not more evident than it was during the debate process.

There were two major debates, and in each one of them I wanted to make sure that the audience understood that there was a clear difference between myself and the other candidates. It was my goal to address issues such as poverty, economic development, and youth development which were very specific to the people of the city and to show that I had real solutions to the problems that they were facing. The first of these debates was at the Averitt Center in downtown Statesboro. Though the crowd was not as large as I had imagined it, all the local news outlets were there along with each candidate's support team. The reporters busied themselves by bouncing between the candidates taking turns interviewing them. In this process, a young reporter from Georgia Southern University mustered up the courage to ask me the question that seemed to be the 800-pound gorilla in the room. "What is like being the only African American candidate in the race and possibly the first African American Mayor of the city?" I was a little thrown off by the question but was not shocked. Throughout the race there was a lot of buzz around the fact that the city was on the verge of electing its first female mayor as she had become the clear favorite to win with myself and the incumbent a close second. During the race, I walked the question of race very carefully as I knew that our community still had a way to go as it related to this matter. So, in a solid pivot, inserted a quick joke about being unaware of the matter and refocused the conversation to my preparedness to serve in the role and my ideas about moving the city forward. In hindsight, I believe that decision was best as it really allowed me to bring some light to the issues that the city was facing and how policy could bring about real change within our city.

Though this was not my first time running for a city seat, this night was the first time that the greater city was introduced to Jonathan McCollar. As the moderator reeled off his questions, it became clear that I was a candidate that was very serious about policy and had real solutions to the problems that our city faced. In fact, I was the only candidate that had put forth a platform that laid out a vision for the city.

When the debate ended, I made sure to circulate through the room and shake the hands of as many people as I possibly could. While doing so, I ran into a couple that stayed behind so they could ask me a few questions. As I reeled off answers to their volley of questions, I became a little puzzled by the exchange, as polite and pleasant as it was. Then, in a moment of full disclosure the husband stated that he and his wife entered the debate supporting one candidate but were leaving as a supporter of the People Over Politics Movement. In this moment it had become apparent that more people than not were tired of politics as usual and desired a real change.

As the race went on, we continued to grow in numbers and in strength. By the time the second debate rolled around in October, I could look into the crowd from the stage and see that there were more faces of support than there were in the last debate. However, there was a face in the crowd that stood out to me more so than any other. It was the face of a young law enforcement officer for the city of Statesboro. I am not sure as to why he resonated with me during this debate, but it was clear that he was paying close attention to every word that was being said on that stage. His demeanor remained calm yet focused throughout the event. Even while on stage answering questions, I could not help but wonder what he was thinking as he clearly understood that his very livelihood would be in the hands of one of those individuals on the stage.

When the debate ended it was my intention to make my way to him to pick his brain for a few thoughts, but before I could get to him, I was stopped for questions from some citizens and media representatives. Luckily, he made his way over to my wife and stated to her that this race was a no brainer and it was clear who should be the next mayor of the city. When she shared this story with me, she stated that his concern lay mostly in the fact that too many people in general were not yet ready to address the issue of poverty head on. He knew that his job as a law enforcement officer dealt too often with folks in the worst moments of their lives and until we were able to truly address poverty and the cascading ills that are associated with it then his job will be that much harder. As I listened, I knew that he was right because during that time period, like now, too many politicians find it easier to prepare law enforcement officers for war than to actually address the needs of the environment that they are sending them in. As a result, the populous and law enforcement are forced to navigate the complexities of politically motivated policies versus getting solutions to the issues they are facing.

In the weeks leading up to election night we pounded the streets working to get as many people to the polls as possible. It was refreshing to see the energy surrounding the election. It seemed that everywhere you turned there was a sign or bumper sticker supporting this or that candidate. We did not know what the future held, but we knew that history was going to be made one way or another. The city was about to elect its first female mayor, or it was going to elect its first African American mayor.

The morning of the election I awoke early and went out to put up signs at the polling stations. I remember having a sense of calm as I believed that I had done all I could do. Throughout the day we made calls and social media postings to encourage people to go to the polls. In every call we made there was always a friendly voice on the other end reassuring us that they were going to make it their business to get to the polling station.

When the polls closed, we immediately went out to pick up our signage. Meanwhile, my wife and a few other volunteers went to the elections office to monitor the numbers as they came in. She would call periodically to update me as I busied myself with my task of picking up my signage from across the city as I worked off nervous energy.

Once I completed picking up the signs, I made my way to the elections' office. I arrived just in time for the final numbers to come in. It seemed like it took them forever to put them up, but like a bell in the night a voice rang out saying, "There's a run-off!" It seemed as if God had answered my prayers. This is what I wanted. I wanted the opportunity to go head to head with the leading candidate, Jan Moore, and show the city that there was a difference between the two of us. I wanted to show the city that I was a candidate that had taken the time to put together a platform that laid out a vision for all of the people of the city and that I was going to work tirelessly to improve the quality of life for all of the people that call Statesboro home.

That night there was so much excitement in the air. We stopped by a gas station and the horns were blowing with excitement. You would have thought that we had won the election. However, I understood exactly why there was so much excitement. It was because for the first time many people in the city felt that there was a chance for them to get representation that was going to look out for their best interest as well. They too had become believers of the People Over Politics movement.

Over the next few weeks, we hit the streets harder than ever. We had seen the runoff strategy before and understood that my opponents believed that those that supported our campaigns would not come back out for a runoff election. However, this time as we hit the doors, we had absentee ballot applications in tow. We believed that if we had a chance to win this race then we would have to increase the expected turnout numbers by leaving no stones unturned.

It seemed like the weeks leading up to election night were a blur or at best some form of Groundhog's day. We hit the doors every single day. We worked at a feverish pace encouraging the people to go to the polls while outlining that this is our opportunity for real change within our city. This message had been taken to heart and we believed that we were on the verge of bringing real change to our beloved city.

Election day rolled around, and we were back out putting up signs early that morning. There was a sense of optimism in the air. We ran our plan well and had a real chance of winning. Throughout the day, we monitored the numbers, made calls and social media postings. By the end of the day, all our data led us to believe that we could win by a very small margin even with the consideration of being behind on the early vote.

When the polls closed, we went out to pick up the signs. I can recall the nervous energy running through my body as I felt that in this moment, I was the dog that chased cars and had finally caught one. Then, my phone rang. It was my wife. I picked it up and she went on to report that it was close, and we were waiting for the city's largest precinct to come in. My heart sank, I continued to busy myself with the busy work of collecting the election signs.

As we finished, my volunteer left, and I sat alone in the parking lot trying to wrap my mind around what was about to happen. As I sat there, it seemed as if there were a million thoughts racing through my mind. And then, with a piercing blare my phone rang. It was my wife. The final numbers had come in and we had lost by 93 votes. As I hung up tears began to flow down my cheeks. Not because I lost the race, but because I had let the entire city down. I believed I let down the unemployed single mother who walked with me nearly every day with her children in tow knocking on hundreds of doors. I believed I had let down the students that I taught and the elderly woman who said she could see God walking with us. This unbearable weight seemed as if it was crushing my soul and taking the very life out of me. We had done all the right things to win and to bring about change, yet we still lost.

After pulling myself together, I went to meet the team at the election's office. As I pulled up, I could see them outside huddled in a group. We all hugged each other, and I proceeded to enter the building. I looked at the numbers and wondered what else we could have done to win this race. Then a familiar monotone voice said to me, "Jonathan, you ran a good race." As I turned, I could see that it was the voice of the county's elections supervisor. I said, "Thank you." But I found it odd that these words would be coming from her as she has always had a negative disposition towards me in the past.

For days I was down on myself and was heartbroken as I still carried the weight of believing that I had let down the entire city. However, I could not shake the encounter with the election's supervisor. So, one day I stopped by the elections office to review the numbers from the race. As I sat there, I was unclear as to what I was looking for, but I knew that if there was going to be something there then it would be in the data.

While waiting for the data, I made idle conversation with the staff members. After a short wait, a young lady returned with the information. I said my goodbyes and made my way out. When I got into my car I began to pour through the pages and like an 800-pound gorilla in a room there it was. Over the course of the runoff campaign, we collected close to 200 absentee ballot applications. And of the 200 applications, 141 of them were denied. When I inquired about the reason for the rejection, the staff shared with me that they were rejected due to the Georgia Exact Match law.

At this time in Georgia, county elections offices had the ability to reject an absentee ballot if they concluded that a signature did not match exactly to what they had on file. This is a very subjective process that threatens the very fabric of our democracy. This is especially true in a case like Bulloch County because any person that's native to this community can look at an address and tell you how this person is likely to vote and their race. I shared this information with the campaign team, they sat in awe as they knew that had those applications been granted, we could have won the race by as many as 48 votes. There was no doubt in our minds that in the 2013 race we were the latest victims of a suppressive voter system that was inundated with flawed and subjective policies.

CHAPTER XI - WE ARE THE DIFFERENCE

In the months following the election, it seemed as though all hell broke loose in America. Across every social media platform, you heard about case after case of unarmed Black people being killed unjustly. Whether it was Mike Brown, Sandra Bland, Tamir Rice, Eric Garner, or the Charleston 9 the stories all seemed to have the common thread of a life being lost to a senseless act of violence fueled by an ignorant social construct. However, if there were two cases that truly broke my heart, I would have to say that they would be the cases of Tamir Rice and the Charleston 9.

Tamir Rice was a 12-year-old who lived in Cleveland, Ohio. While he was out playing in the park across from his home with a toy gun, a 911 call was made to report that a black male was in the park pulling a gun on people. Within two seconds of the arrival of the local law enforcement officers, Tamir had been shot and killed. The life of a child had ended in a flash.

As I watched this story unfold on TV, I could not help but think that this could have been one of my sons in this park. Even now, the mere thought of this sends chills through my body. I can't imagine what it was like for the parents and family members of Tamir to get the news that their young one had been taken away from them. This innocent child's life was stolen while playing in a park across the street from his home. A place where every child should feel safe, but due to the dysfunctional socialization of the American populous, as it relates to race, even a child with black skin at play is perceived as a threat.

In June of 2015, three hours away from where I live, nine lives were senselessly taken while in their home church of Emanuel Methodist Episcopal Church in Charleston, SC. In this incident, Dylan Roof entered the doors of the church with the intent to murder those inside so he could become a martyr to what he believed as an inevitable race war. In a cold and calculating manner he sat through prayer and Bible study before opening firing on the congregants. As the shots rang out, 9 of the parishioners were fatally wounded in what is now deemed as one of the saddest days in American History.

From 2014 to 2017, these cases were like grenades exploding across the country. Though the nation had seen these types of atrocities before, the difference this time was the invention of social media and the will of the young people not to remain silent. It was through their will that America had to come face to face with its scarlet letter as it relates to race and inclusivity. The voices of young people rang out from shore to shore. We could see them on our TV screens, phones, computers, and every other imaginable means of communication. They were organized. They were diverse. They were loud and they were brave.

It seemed that no community was immune to these young people letting their voices be heard, and my city was no different. The young people in the community were upset with what had been happening across the country and wanted to make sure that their voices were heard. So, they organized a rally on the courthouse lawn to show their solidarity with others across the nation. In doing so, they asked several people from the community to come and speak to the participants, and I was lucky enough to be asked to do so.

I had spent a lot of time working with many of these young people on different projects and had grown attached to them. However, the one that stands out in this matter the most is the daughter of a close cousin of mine. This was a young lady that I had watched grow over the years from being a great student, cheerleader, and track team member to entering her early years of college and now a community activist in her own right. So, it came as no surprise to me that she helped organize this rally.

I arrived at the rally late as I was traveling from out of town due to a work matter. When I arrived, the courthouse lawn was filled with young people from across the community and in the shadows were those ever-supporting elders. As I stepped out of my car, I could fill the energy in the air as a light misty rain fell on the faces of those in attendance. Rushing to make my way through the crowd, I could hear the voices of young leaders expressing their heartbreak about the senseless murders of unarmed people across the country.

When I stepped on the stage, I was greeted by several of the students, community leaders, and my little cousin. I listened to the fire in the bellies of the young people as they spoke. Then, it was my turn. As I took one final glance back before speaking, a sign that read, "AM I Next?", caught my eye. When I looked up, I saw that it was being held by my little cousin, Kierra, who was a student at Georgia Southern at the time. Tears welled up in my eyes and my voice cracked, but a fire stirred in me that night like none before. Until this day, I can't tell you what I said but I do know that in that moment I was able to connect to those young people like never. When I finished, I caught a glance of the mayor. She was supposed to speak after me, but that never happened. For the life of me, I will never be able to understand how an elected official can remain silent when so many of the people that they lead are in pain. That will never be the case for me as I understand that injustice prevails when the just souls remain silent.

Following that rally, my spirit felt restless. I knew I could be doing more to move our community, state, and nation forward. I continued to work in the community and volunteer on campaigns, but I was still seeking that transformative experience that would push me to grow. Then, in the summer of 2016 my wife, our good friend Ivory, and I were elected to become delegates to the 2016 Democratic National Convention in Philadelphia, PA.

Leading up to our departure for Philadelphia for the convention I had some excitement about it, but I was pretty much treating it like any other convention that I have attended in the past. However, upon my arrival I quickly realized that the DNC was totally different from anything other convention I had been a part of. The entire energy of the city was abuzz about the DNC and its delegates being there. Everywhere we went we were treated with so much love. With us being true southerners, we relished in the feeling and returned the love every time we had the chance.

The convention was held at the Wells Fargo Center. There, every who's who of Democratic politics was in attendance along with as many Hollywood faces as you could imagine. We were able to meet the late great Elijah Cummings and have great conversation with Congressman John Lewis as we sat with the Georgia delegation. By happenstance, I struck up a nice conversation with a young woman and even took a picture with her that was photobombed by Chris Hayes for MSNBC. What I didn't know at the time, but was later informed by my wife, was that I was talking to Rosario Dawson who happens to be one of my favorite actresses.

Amid this convention was the contentious debate of the results of the primary. Seemingly, we were all there to crown Hillary as the winner and our choice to take on then candidate Donald J. Trump. However, the Bernie delegates cried foul in the process and refused to go quietly into the night. I could not help but be in awe at the level of passion and commitment that they had for their candidate and their cause. If it had not been for them the Democratic party would not have had its progressive platform for the 2016 election.

Night after night we heard riveting speeches from politicians, celebrities, activists, and American icons. The speech that moved me the most came from the Rev. Dr. William Barber out of North Carolina. Re. Barber is not only a minister, but a political activist who had shed light on the immorality of poverty. In his speech he made it plain that poverty was the greatest threat that we were facing as a nation and that it was a tremendous threat to how we defined humanity.

As I listened to Rev. Barber's speech, I could not help but to think back on my hometown and ponder the issues that we were facing. It became abundantly clear that every major issue that we were facing had its roots in poverty. It did not matter whether it was the growth of gangs, violent crimes, petty crimes, or economic instability it all came back to one thing, poverty. In years prior to this moment, I participated in deep conversations around poverty and had worked on crafting policy and community plans to address it. However, for the first time, I was given the messaging tools to better communicate the severity of the matter.

After we returned from the convention, I was charged and ready to make a change in our city with what I believed as the necessary tools for success. However, I felt that something was missing in my toolkit. On the outside, it seemed that everything was there, but I knew it needed to be more. The thing that I was missing was the great sacrifice for the cause. I was missing the thing that was going to truly test everything that I believed in. Then as fate would have it, a friend posted a job opportunity for a company that was working on a presidential campaign. I inboxed him and inquired about the opportunity. He told me that he believed that I would be a great candidate for the job and advised me to send them my resume. So, I did.

When I sent in my credentials, I was not expecting to be reached out to as I have applied for similar roles before and did not hear anything from the organizations. That was not the case in this instance. A few hours after submitting my information I received a phone call from the organization. After several discussions over the next few hours, I was presented with what

I believed an opportunity that was too good to pass up. After speaking with my wife, I accepted the position, resigned from my role at East Georgia State College and was on the road to Raleigh, NC two days later.

I had no idea what to expect when I arrived in the Raleigh office on that Monday morning in September of 2016. When I walked in it was busied with staff members printing and rushing items and people out of the door. It was one of the most chaotic scenes I had ever seen. After stumbling through my first day, I was told that I would be transferring to the Durham office for the remainder of my time there. The next day I awoke bright and early and made my way to Durham. When I stepped foot into the office, it was abundantly clear that there was a real difference between the two offices. The chaos was still there, but it was an organized chaos. It was a chaos that was spearheaded by who I have come to believe is a political mad scientist, Scott.

Scott is an author, political guru, and probably one of the most genuine individuals that I had ever met. He was from Denver, Colorado, and he and several of his friends made the trek to North Carolina to be a part of this historic campaign. They were a rag tag group of friends, but they were more than loyal to each other. More than that they were especially loyal to Scott. At that time, I did not understand why, but the mystery was not going to last long for me as to why they valued him so.

Over the next few days, I inundated myself in the work and the cause. I learned the reporting systems and technology associated with the campaign. I learned the payroll system flawlessly and even upped my familiarity with Apple products which is big for me because I am an Android person. I worked to build relationships with the staff and the canvassers who went into the community every day. I submersed myself into everything that was related to the operations of that campaign.

In its peak, our operation was sending more than one hundred people into the field every day. To say that this was an amazing feat by a great team would be an understatement. What was most astonishing was that the canvassers and the staff all came from different walks of life. We had retired educators, healthcare professionals, service sector employees, and countless more. We had individuals who slept in homeless shelters at night and were the first to work and the last to leave. However, of all the people that I engaged with, the person who stands out to me the most was Mike.

Mike was one of the most popular people on the team. When he walked into the building the staffers and canvassers just lit up. Every time that you would see him, he would have this infectious smile on his face. I never understood why until I heard his story. Mike was always a popular guy in Durham with a Robin Hood type of reputation. It turned out that he was a big drug dealer in the city prior to coming to work for us. And it was during this time that he would spend tons of money on doing things for the kids in the neighborhood. He did everything from back to school events to simply just helping mothers in need. However, that all came to an end when he was arrested and served time in jail.

When Mike came to us, he was looking for a way to change his life around. He wanted to know what it felt like to be a part of something that was positive and working to build the community in a very different way. However, when he filled out the application to become a part of the team, he did not believe that he would ever be hired because of his past transgressions. Until this day I have no idea as to how he got hired, but he did. His gratefulness to be a part of the team showed in everything that he did for the campaign. He was the first show up and the last to leave most days. On many of these days, he and I would have short but in-depth conversations about life, changing the community, and many other things. However, the bulk of his conversation was centered around the fact that he believed that he had been given a second chance on life.

Through this experience, I learned that anyone could be used as an instrument for change within their community. I saw people who believed themselves to be hopeless under any other circumstances gleaming with the thoughts of being able to make an honest wage and a difference in their community. And to me, this spoke volumes as to what it meant to truly be an American.

As rewarding as it was to be a part of the North Carolina experience, it was also just as disheartening at times. It had become a routine to get calls from canvassers letting us know that they were being harassed by local citizens and, at times, local law enforcement. Some folks were enraged by the mere presence of the canvassers in their neighborhoods. And as a result, these residents would use racial slurs towards the canvassers, call law enforcement on them and in one case sling dog feces on one of them. As I would take these calls, it had become clear that we were on the frontlines of a political race that was tinged by the American sin of racism and otherness.

Through this experience I noticed an absence of hope and the fundamental belief that America's best days are in front of her. In these moments, I realized that hope was the most powerful campaign tool that any candidate or person in leadership could possibly have as it fueled the imagination of those who followed about what things could be. I also learned that fear candidates tend to be incompetent candidates that lack vision, real leadership skills and solutions to the problems people are facing. This was something that I vowed that I would never be.

When Election Day 2016 rolled around I was mentally exhausted from working nearly sixty straight days of twelve plus hour shifts for the campaign. In the last days leading up to election night, we went from a team that was turning out more than one hundred canvassers a day into the field to sending out a little more than twenty. The writing on the wall was clear by this time and it read that Donald J. Trump was going to take the great State of North Carolina. He, like Obama, had inspired voters to engage in a process that they had grown apathetic to. Meanwhile, Hillary was in an uphill battle in a state where voter suppression was real and election day voter machines were rampantly malfunctioning in cities that were Democratic strongholds.

That night, as I sat in a Red Lobster, I watched the tv screens as the first of the numbers began rolling in. Even in my exhausted state, I could not help but feel the energy of the onlookers as they waited for each state to be called. I, wanting to be hopefully optimistic, watched, but understood that there were too many states that were polling too close for Hillary to win the Electoral College. I finished my food, drove to the place I was staying, and went to sleep knowing that when I awoke the next day that Donald Trump was going to be the next President of the United States of America.

CHAPTER XII - ALL IN

When I returned from North Carolina, I was very focused on the steps it would take for me to become the next mayor of Statesboro. I began to organize immediately and held the first campaign meeting in my home in the month of December of 2016. At this meeting, there was a mixture of people from the community. There were local business owners, faculty and staff from the local university, retirees and close family and friends. This meeting was primarily made up of the people that were a part of the first campaign for mayor or supported it.

When the meeting ended, I felt positive about it, but I believed that we needed to expand our campaign. I began to reach out to some people that were not necessarily close friends at the time, but individuals that I recognized as having the same outlook on many different matters. A series of small meetings began to occur over the next several months. It was in these meetings where I was able to gain a lot more insight into the people that were now becoming a part of the People Over Politics movement.

On August 25, 2017 I walked into City Hall with my wife and our good friend Ivory to declare myself as a candidate for Mayor of the city of Statesboro. My heart raced as I sat at the desk of the City Clerk and filled out the necessary paperwork to become a candidate for the office. To my back stood my wife Adrianne and Ivory. They took photos and smiled throughout the process. They knew that I was a little nervous, but they gave me the comfort and strength that I needed in that moment.

When we left the building, it had begun to drizzle a little, but we felt it was important to address the city. We stood under a little awning as it rained and went live on Facebook to announce to the city that it was official that we were going to make another run for Mayor. In this address I wanted to make sure that residents knew that I recognized that poverty was the biggest issue that we were facing and that I was going to work diligently to fight it and all of the ills that were associated with it.

To say we hit the ground running is an understatement. We tore through neighborhood after neighborhood working to gain support for what we believed to be one of the most significant political races in the history of our city. The fight, as we saw it, was to determine whether our city was going to step into its future with a new vision and a new commitment to its people or continue with the status quo. A status quo that had left more than fifty percent of its population in poverty, no investment into its young people, and a recreational program with little funding by the city in nearly two decades.

We were a broad coalition of people from all walks of life. Our ranks were made up of local business owners, professors, single moms, grandparents, and the like. We were also Black, White, Hispanic, Asian, Gay, Straight, Christian, and more. I felt that we had put together a team that reflected the diversity of our community and was committed to moving our city forward. We were a proud and hard-working group dedicated to a cause that was much bigger than ourselves.

I can't put into words how powerful it was for us to go into neighborhoods and talk with the people firsthand about the issues that they were facing. These conversations ranged from young mothers concerned about the needs of their children to fathers that made just enough to put food on the table for their families. We also heard the stories of how the people felt left out and behind.

While out canvassing in a local apartment complex, a member of the team ran into an old student of mine. As she talked with him about supporting the campaign, he shared with her that he knew me and was an old student. They continued to talk, and he began to share with her that he had fallen into some hard situations and had made some bad decisions here and there along the way. She felt that it would be a good idea if he spoke with me, so she quickly came over to where I was to let me know that there was a young man who needed to speak with me. She pointed me in his direction, and I was off to meet up with him.

When I headed over to the young man, I immediately saw that it was the adult version of little Rashad. One of my favorite students. He was a good kid who had gone through a very tough life. His mother had died while he was still very young, and it was clear that he had a hard time processing her death.

Rashad and I talked for a while. He shared with me some of the things that he was going through and how he felt that nobody cared about people in his situation. As I listened, I could not help but hear the same young man who sat in my class all those years ago. It became clear that in that moment, Rashad did not need me as a politician or as someone that was going to wag his finger at him. In that moment Rashad needed a human being who was willing to listen to him and to recognize the importance of human contact. When our conversation came to an end, I left a little piece of my heart with him as I could only imagine how many more Rashads there were in our community.

In the days and weeks that followed, we continued to knock on doors and to share our story and vision with whoever would listen. With each day that passed, it seemed that our campaign grew stronger and stronger. Our social media feeds began to fill up with people sharing their stories about us coming to the homes and talking with them about the future of our city. For many of them, it was the first time that any candidate ever came by to show any interest in them supporting their campaign. This excited us as it became clear that we were beginning to inspire people that had never been a part of the process to become engaged in what was happening in their very own city.

When the night of the first debate rolled around, there was an energy in the room that could be felt. This debate was hosted by Agape Worship Center, a local church within the community. The event was moderated by now Georgia State President for the NAACP Rev. James "Major" Woodall and a young woman from the community and the timekeeper was now the Bulloch County Chapter President of the NAACP, Delinda Gaskins. The event was filled with some great questions and an audience that hung on every word that flowed from the candidate mouths.

By the end of the debate, the room was charged from the energy of our supporters and those who had been swayed to join the People Over Politics movement. In the midst of this excitement a young local attorney made his way over to me and plainly asked, "What is the difference in the campaign since the last race?". Admittedly, I was a little thrown off by the question because I was not expecting it and truthfully had not given it any thought. However, after a brief reflection, I responded simply that I get to be me in this race.

What I have come to learn is that the American people are not looking for those who represent them flawlessly. What the people are looking for out of their representatives is for them to be honest and authentic, and this is what I was able to do within this campaign. I was able to provide an honest vision and was able to speak plainly and truthfully about the issues our community was facing. So, when asked, do I believe that my city is the best city in the world? I could plainly answer yes, but I do believe that there are areas that we could do a better job on to make us that much better.

After the debate, the county fair rolled into town. I can't think of too many events that are more American than your hometown's county fair and the big parade that comes with it in Statesboro. Each year, on the opening day of the fair, the parade marches down South Main Street to the cheers of the local citizens and those who made their way over from the surrounding counties.

I knew that this was going to be a great opportunity for us to show off our level of support and to touch some people that we had yet to have the opportunity to reach. Prior to the event we made signs and banners. We went to Walmart and bought what I believed to be all the candy that the store had along with balloons and several helium tanks. It was our intent to give every child along the way just a little something for them to take with them and to remember us by.

When it was our turn to hit the main strip, we were ready. We marched along waving our hands, giving hugs, and loading up the kids with plenty of balloons and candy. I dived into the crowd passing out hugs and handshakes while trying to make my way to every person who called my name. The energy of the parade was amazing and the team of people that worked to make it a success are beyond any words that I can imagine.

When the parade came to an end there was the murmuring amongst the group that I was unaware of as we were walking the parade route. Apparently, the then sitting mayor was in the parade just ahead of us and chose not to get out of her truck and just wave from afar. Some of the energy that we were receiving came from people in attendance who were happy to see a candidate that was willing to come out and meet them face to face while passing out hugs and genuine smiles.

I learned in that moment that the people wanted leadership that was willing to engage them. For too long in our city a large portion of the population felt disconnected from the people who were representing them. In fact, they believed that their leaders did not care about them and they, the people, had grown apathetic towards city hall.

I wish that I could pretend that I did not know what they were talking about, but I knew all too well. On the west and north sides of the city, the neighborhoods were plagued by dilapidated homes, poor roads, the lack of sidewalks, and the lack of necessary infrastructure to mitigate the rainwater to prevent flooding. These neighborhoods also lacked adequate social infrastructure and programming for the youth. As a result, the trust in those who represented them had eroded to near nothing and so morale of the people was low. Comparatively, I am of the school of thought that neighborhoods, like the ones that make up the north and west side of the city, are the byproduct of poor policy and the failure of governing bodies to garner or allocate the funding necessary for a city's balanced growth. In short, poor neighborhoods are not the reflection of the people who live in them, but of those politicians in decision making positions who fail to invest into the quality of life of those that call these areas home.

Following the parade there was a clear shift in momentum in this race. For the first time, our campaign had become mainstream and the people of the city began to believe that we had a chance of unseating a popular mayor. Nonetheless, we remained focused and continued to put out signs, host community events, knock on doors, and tell our story everywhere we went. And during all of this, our team continued to grow, and our volunteer numbers were skyrocketing. We went from having one to two canvassers to fielding ten to twelve canvassers at a time. The People Over Politics Movement was real and had taken on a voice that was much bigger than me becoming the mayor of the city of Statesboro. This could not have been any more evident than when I fell ill one day while out canvassing.

One Saturday, during the early voting period, I planned a canvassing event for the team and was out in the community. While hitting the doors in the neighborhood, I began to feel a little ill, but I was determined to complete the task. I continued through my normal routine and met additional volunteers in the field. I had strategically identified the area that I wanted to canvass for the day and dutifully passed out the assignments to the volunteers. We started talking to the residents about the campaign and its vision for the people. We shared how we wanted to bring about real change to our city and institute leadership that was going to represent the city in its entirety.

As the time passed, large beads of sweat began to roll down my head and I grew weaker with every step. I began to verbalize to the team that I was not feeling well and that we may need to call it an early day. However, this group of volunteers were not on board with stopping. They told me repeatedly that they had this and for me to go home, but I refused the idea of leaving them in the field without me. When they saw that I was not going to leave they called my wife and long story short, I was on my way home. Through the course of that day, they not only continued to knock on doors in the neighborhoods that we had identified but went into several other additional neighborhoods. By the time they had finished they touched nearly three times the people and area I intended. Instantly, I understood that the People Over Politics movement was much bigger than Jonathan McCollar: its voice belonged solely to the people.

When we kicked off this campaign we focused so much on strategy and putting a mayor into office who was going to govern with the best interest of all the people in mind. We failed to recognize the most powerful aspect of the movement, hope. Growing up I would hear Jesse Jackson say" Keep Hope Alive", never understanding what the power of hope really meant to the people and their ability to overcome difficult situations. Hope is that thing that causes you to believe in a better day even when all the days before were unbearable. And it was hope that came to our city.

As the days drew nearer to the election, we would knock on doors and people would tell us that they had already voted for us or that there had been some form of a meeting and the entire neighborhood was planning to vote for our campaign. We would log into social media and see flyers made by people who were never interested in politics before now supporting our campaign. We saw college students, professors, pastors, average Joes and Janes, and people from all walks of life coming together. There were so many people declaring their support that it almost became overwhelming to think that this small rag tag group of people could bring about so much change, fire, and energy to one community.

During the campaign, we noticed a few college students joining our ranks. At first it was two-three, but that changed rapidly as election day neared and those numbers began to rise. When it came time for the campus debate, we were impressed to see a high number of students in attendance, especially given that it was a basketball game that night. We were even more surprised to see the number of students supporting our campaign.

In the few talks that I gave on campus prior to this moment, I would ask the question "Is this the generation that we have been waiting for?". And it was always met with silence and awkwardness. However, I refused to stop asking, because I believed that it gave the students a space to walk into and be a part of a movement that was looking to make history in our city. It worked.

During the debate at Georgia Southern University, the students critiqued every word that each candidate said and let it be known whether they agreed or not. This group of students were smart, tough, and understood the issues that affected them the most. They were concerned about police harassment, safety, and creating an environment that enhanced their college experience. They also wanted a city government that was willing to engage them and include them in the decision-making process.

When the debate came to an end the energy in the room was electric. As I left the stage, I was given a hug by one of the moderators and she whispered into my ear how inspired she was by our campaign. What I did not know was that this young woman and I would go on to be great friends and she would become a true inspiration for me.

Tables had been set up in the back of the room for the candidates to meet and greet the students. The goal was to give students some one on one time with each candidate. Unfortunately, the sitting mayor was unable to stay, and this upset the many students who felt that this was a sign that she did take them seriously or did not care about their votes or opinions. This was a feeling that they made clear when they stated that during the debate they felt as if she was talking down to them. In that moment it became clear that it is vitally important to take the time out to genuinely engage every person that you want to represent. I believe it is difficult to adequately represent a person that you are unwilling to engage. That night we stayed until the last student left and the staff eventually had to kick us out.

The last day of early voting had come to an end. And like normal, we were at the election's office collecting the data we needed to strategically plan our next steps heading into the weekend. As we reviewed the numbers, it was clear that the race was extremely close. We believed that we were down by 30-40 votes at the time. This was a good sign because we believed that if we were able to keep the numbers close in the early vote then our Election Day strategy would deliver us a victory.

After reviewing the data, we decided to do one last massive canvassing of the voters one more time before Election Day. That Friday evening, we planned a three-day strategy that would give us the opportunity to touch as many voters as possible. The next day we were up with our t-shirts, clipboards, and handbills knocking on as many doors as possible delivering the gospel of the People Over Politics movement. That Sunday we repeated the process and then brought it to a close that Monday.

Since the start of the election I had been backwards planning what Election Day would look like. It always ended at 7:00 pm with the last volunteer dropping off a voter at the polls. Throughout this process, I would never allow myself to imagine what victory or defeat would look like. I have learned over the years that if you create a good plan, and stick to it, then you have taken care of all the things that you could control and now fate must have the last say.

That Monday before the 2017 election I woke up at 5:00am. I started the day with social media posts and text messages. I knew that these communications may be the last quality touches prior to people casting their votes. So, I wanted to make sure that it was sweet, to the point, and genuine. It took me several hours to complete the task but when it was done, I was satisfied with the positive feedback from the task.

The remainder of the day was spent organizing call sheets, canvassing turfs, and touching base with the volunteers. We worked frantically as we believed that this race was now ours to win or lose. Our front yard began to look like a military staging ground as volunteers parked their cars along the road and pickup trucks with ATVs in tow lined my front yard.

Adrianne and her team organized the data sets while several other volunteers prepped signage and went out to the polling precincts to stage our signs along the roads leading up to the precinct. We understood that most people casting their votes on Election Day already knew who they were going to vote for, but we felt that we needed to make every effort to fight for every vote.

The team worked well into the night. They were making sure that we had dotted every I and crossed every T. When the midnight hour had come and gone, they finally decided to go home and get some rest. However, for me, sleep was not an option as the first Election Day volunteer was scheduled to show up at 2:30am.

Throughout this campaign, individual stories of dedication littered its path. However, Robin, my 2:30am volunteer, personifies the level of sacrifice that so many people had. She is a single mom and a local business owner. She is smart, tough, and strong willed. I knew when she said that she was coming to my house at 2:30am, she meant it.

When the doorbell rang, she, I and another volunteer jumped

into the van and went out to put up additional signage around the city. The task seemed simple, until you realize that 13 square miles is a lot to cover in a short amount of time. We had our system: she would prep them, I would stake them, and the driver kept us rolling. I realized that I could not put into words the level of dedication that people like Robin had made so that we could get to this point. I began to reflect on all the single moms, professors, and many others who would get off work and meet me in the neighborhoods to canvas voters. Knowing all the things that had been sacrificed to get us where we were, added to my determination to do everything humanly possible to win.

At 6:00 am, the second wave of volunteers came in as we were still out putting up signage. Leading the way was April, a professor at the local university who had turned into a beast for the campaign: energetic, determined, and optimistic. She, Adrianne, and several volunteers lead the charge as they began an ambitious Election Day canvassing effort. We did not want to leave any voter behind.

After my team finished placing signage around the city, we rolled into the canvassing effort and morphed into taking people to the polls and phone banking. Then the unexpected happened. It was 11:00 am and we had completed everything we had planned to do. We had knocked on all the doors, made all the calls, and the numbers were not where we needed them to be.

Puzzled and concerned, my mind raced as I thought through all the things that we could possibly do next to save the campaign. Then, in a very inquisitive way, Yevette, a routine campaign volunteer, asked, "Well, what are you going to do?". This simple question was profound. I did not know. A million thoughts ran through my mind. A mind that had been going since 5:00am the day before with no sleep. Then it dawned on me that I needed to blow off some steam and what better to do that than by hopping on one of the ATVs and driving it as fast as it could go.

The revving of the engine gave me power. The adrenaline flowed through my body and my heart began to race. My mind began to clear, and I was able to refocus.

When I returned to headquarters, I had a clear understanding of the next steps. I asked everyone who was not out in the field to go onto their social media pages and send direct messages to everyone that they knew who lived in the city and asked them to go vote and take someone with them. When they completed that task, I asked them to go through their cell phones and do the same. We began to see more and more people make their way to the polls, and the numbers were beginning to slowly trend in the direction that we wanted them to. But then arose another problem.

The phones began to ring with citizens complaining of not being able to vote because the address on their IDs did not match the address on their voter registration card, names not being found in the system, and the refusal to inform them of what number voter they were for the day. At this point, our good friend Ivory reached out to the Georgia Democratic Party for guidance to help us navigate this matter. Meanwhile, it was after noon and I felt that this would be a good time for me and Adrianne to go cast our ballots for the Movement.

When we arrived at the polling site located at the Board of Education there were several dozen people casting their ballots. This was a positive sign for us because we knew that the rush was going to be the after-work crowd. As we made our way through the line, we said our hellos and thanked the people that were sending their best wishes. I purposely used my Georgia Southern ID to see if there was going to be any push back as it doesn't have an address on it. It was not a problem.

Then I made my way down the line to where I was picking up my card to vote and noticed that the election's supervisor was standing there. I asked the volunteer to tell me what number voter I was for the day. The volunteer slowly looked back at the election's supervisor and in a terse tone the election's supervisor scoffed, "Gone'n tell'em!". We calmly waited for the numbers and continued to move forward and cast our ballots.

As seasoned voters and campaigners, we knew most of the rules and understood the process of how elections are supposed to be run. We knew that if we asked what number voter we were, then that information should be shared with us. We knew that if it was a state issued ID then we must be allowed to vote. And we knew that the address on the ID did not matter as some of the acceptable forms of ID lacked an address. However, if you are not engaged in the elections process, beyond casting a vote, then it is easy to see the level of frustration that was presented to our headquarters on Election Day. These acts, and others like them, are the subtle measures of voter suppression that must be continuously addressed as they are the means that many voters become disenfranchised from the democratic process.

When we returned to our headquarters, the room was buzzing with phones ringing, fingers typing and canvassers rushing through the doors and leaving with packets to canvas the neighborhoods. I hopped on one of the ATVs and canvassed nearby neighborhoods by knocking on doors and arranging for people to be taken to the polls. We could begin to feel the energy in the streets. As we rode by, we could see the hands and hear the yells from the passersby. We now believed that this race was ours to win or lose. We continued to pour into the work while moving at a frantic pace across the city.

As the day went on our number of volunteers continued to swell. The look of determination covered their faces as they believed that we were on the precipice of bringing real change to the city of Statesboro. Amongst these volunteers was my good friend, Trent. He was a congressional candidate earlier that year for Georgia's 12th Congressional District. He and his whole team barged through the doors, grabbed some canvassing material, and started canvassing the neighborhoods. They were tired from the day and were still dressed in their work clothes, but they were hell bent on seeing a real change in our city.

Between four and five o'clock that day my phone rang. It was Holly. Holly is a family friend and one of the sweetest people you could ever meet. She was new to the political scene so when she asked what she could do I tried to keep it simple because I didn't want to scare her away. As asked, she was calling to give me an update from one of the precincts. In a very excited but controlled tone, she told me that the numbers were looking much better than expected. She believed that we were polling at about forty percent. I quickly dismissed these numbers as her being a newcomer filled optimism. We had this conversation twice more and each time she repeated the same thing until she finally stopped me in mid conversation, during our 6:30 call, and said, "Look, I am telling you that you are polling at forty percent easily here." My heart sank because that had put us beyond the numbers we were projecting. I knew then that if those numbers continued in that direction, I was more than likely going to be the next Mayor of Statesboro.

As the polls came to a close, I made my way over to the largest precinct, which was at the Board of Education and sat on the far side of the parking lot and watched as the voters poured in and out of the building. Car after car turned into the parking lot with occupants racing through the doors to get their last-minute votes in. At 6:58 pm I saw my cousin Lyn's car pull up to the front door of the precinct. Her sister Marshay jumped out of the car and ran into the building. She was the last person to cast her ballot for our campaign at that precinct. Even in this moment, I still did not want to celebrate too soon as I did not want to let the people that had sacrificed so much for this campaign down.

When 7 o'clock came we returned to the headquarters. You could feel the excitement in the air. I watched as my cousin Lynn carried April through the doors as she had walked until her legs began to cramp. Yet and still, I was not going to count my chickens before the eggs hatched. I immediately left to head to the election's office to watch as the numbers came in. As I was getting into the car, Scott, a local report and photographer for the newspaper asked if he could go with us. I paused and asked him if we had won. He did not respond.

When I arrived at the election's office, Ivory, my campaign manager was already there watching for the numbers as they came in. I walked over to her and she showed me the current results and we were down by just a few votes in the early numbers. Knowing that we had hit our numbers for the day, I whispered into her ear that I believed that we might have won. And in a classic Ivory voice, she said, "I believe so, too."

The campaign team was calling my phone uncontrollably. They report the numbers from each precinct. With three candidates in the race, we received over forty percent of the vote from one precinct and nearly seventy percent from another precinct. When we combined the numbers, it had become clear that the city of Statesboro had just made history. The only thing we were waiting for were the official results to come into the elections office. When the numbers came out, we reviewed them, and it was official: We had garnered nearly fifty three percent of the total vote. The People Over Politics Campaign had WON!!!!

I rushed outside of the elections office and succumbed to my emotions as tears flowed from my eyes and I cried in joy while praising God. Ivory, being the friend that she has always been, hugged me and whispered gently "We did it." I got on the phone and called Adrianne to let her and the campaign team know that we had won. We could hear the roar from the campaign headquarters, a little less than a mile away, all the way up to the election's office. It felt as if a great burden had been lifted off the city and its people.

When we made it back to headquarters, the team met us in the parking lot with cheers, hugs, and kisses. Then, like a parade, the people came rushing to the campaign headquarters from across the city like none before. They all were overcome with joy and emotion. Some were in tears and others were filled with laughter. We stayed in the parking lot well beyond midnight embracing every emotion that that moment brought us. We knew that the People Over Politics Movement had brought real change to our beloved city.

EPILOGUE

On January 2, 2018 I was sworn into office before a standing room only crowd. I can still hear the applause of the audience as I said the last words of my oath and made my way back to my seat as the new Mayor of the City of Statesboro. There is no doubt that this was one of the proudest days of my life. To be able to look into the tear-filled eyes of family and friends and say that we did it brings on emotions that could never be expressed in words.

When I assumed my role as mayor of my beloved hometown, I understood that it was not going to be an easy task. I was a candidate that did not have the backing of the typical king makers of the city and I recognized that for many my race was still going to be an issue. However, I hung my hat on the belief that our city's best days were in front of it and that most people that call Statesboro home believed in the power of all of us working together to make it a better place for all of us. What I was not prepared for was the amount of resistance that I would receive from the council and staff.

When I was elected, I recognized that I was becoming a part of a team of people who all endorsed the incumbent except one. Understanding this, I immediately reached out to all of them acknowledging this and told them all that I was open and ready to work with them. When I communicated this message, it was my hope that this was going to be an easy fix to an awkward situation. It was not.

From day one, one council member made it his business to oppose and lay barriers to every initiative that I supported. His overzealous behavior was laced with untruths, conspiracy theories, and staff tampering. His actions did not just stay within the corridors of city hall but bled into the community. Despite all his actions, the council managed to support the things that were going to move our city forward the most. In hindsight, I now thank him for all his actions as they have made me a much better mayor. It was through this experience that I learned that it was exponentially important to adhere to the virtues that you hold closest to you. My belief in honesty, transparency, fact-based decisions, and staying above the political fray really played well in my ability to help guide our city through some of the most difficult times in its history.

During the first two years of my administration it became abundantly clear that if we were going to truly move this city forward, I was going to have to build out a pipeline of initiatives that addressed the needs of the people. In this process I, along with several dedicated folks, worked to establish commissions that addressed inclusion excellence, workforce development, and youth development. I understood that it would be through this framework that we would be able to begin the process of addressing some very difficult issues within our community that acted as barriers to us being the community that I knew we ought to be. The establishment of these commissions built the infrastructure to address what I deemed as soft items as they focused on people-oriented matters. However, the city was dealing with several other issues that were eating away at its core.

The first of these issues were the fact the city was dealing with an aging infrastructure system. Many parts of the city would flood during those famous Southern summer thunderstorms. In fact, one year on my wife's birthday our home was completely flooded during one of these episodes. Though we were fortunate in our instance, there have been families that were not so lucky.

The second matter that the city had was that many of the roads were crumbling. In a conversation with the then city manager during our transition period, he estimated that with the city's current budget it would take the city an estimated 50 years to address the needs of the city as it relates to its roads. Understanding the importance of a city's infrastructure and its economic growth, I, along with a fellow council member, worked to mend a damaged relationship with our county government so we would be able to present a T-Splost package to the citizenry for their approval. As a result of this work, the people of the city and the county passed our T-Splost initiative and both the city and the county are repairing and resurfacing roads at an historic rate while building long overdue sidewalks in neighborhoods across the city and establishing a public transportation system. The additional plus in this matter is that many of these projects are done by local contractors which means as we rebuild our community, we are helping small local businesses and creating jobs.

When I came into office there were great projects in the works. The Blue Mile is one of these projects. The Blue Mile is the corridor that connects downtown Statesboro to the gates of our beloved Georgia Southern University. Over the years, this one-mile strip began to deteriorate due to the economic shift in the city. Once famous eateries and thriving businesses became eyesores. So, a group of dedicated folks and organizations came together and started the initiative to fix up this once beloved and thriving area. This effort was catapulted by a $1 million prize for placing third in the 2017 America's Best Communities competition.

The Blue Mile project has also morphed into an effort to provide workforce housing in the neighborhoods along its corridor. It is fueled by a great Homes for Heroes program and the philanthropic efforts of a local developer. It's vision now includes a waterfront area that will create a new state park and economic hub for the city on South Main street. Amid all this great work, I believed that there was a greater vision to chase.

While many parts of the city were seeing extreme amounts of progress, the older neighborhoods in the city were being left behind. These were the areas that were most vulnerable to flooding, poorly maintained roads, excessive numbers of dilapidated housing, and lacked sidewalks in highly traveled areas. These areas were also overlooked when it came to regular maintenance such as mowing the right of ways and tree trimming. On a ride through with the then city manager, I took him to an area where the grass was as tall as the stop sign. He wanted to explain it away as it was due to our area being in a rainy season, but I quickly corrected him and told him it was because this area was being overlooked in so many words.

Early into my administration it became abundantly clear that something had to be done to address the problem of deteriorating neighborhoods. After some research and consultation with Dr. Jermaine Durham, the Director for the Georgia Initiative for Community Housing, it was quite evident that becoming a part of its next cohort had to be a top priority for the city. So, with a new city manager in place we recruited community volunteers and submitted our application for consideration. Late in the fall of 2019, we were notified that we were members of the 2020 cohort for the Georgia Initiative for Community Housing. Out of this action, the city is now aggressively working to revitalize neighborhoods across the city and the parks that serve them.

Suffice it to say, that my administration has been filled with firsts. I am the city's first African American Mayor. Charles Penny is the City's first African American City Manager. Layne Phillips is the city's first public information officer. However, there was a glass ceiling that I believed must be broken and that was the fact that in the city's two hundred plus year history it has never had a woman serve on its council.

In the fall of 2019, there were three council seats up for re-election. There was a lot of buzz around the city about who was going to run and was not. In this process, I would get periodic calls and requests for meetings. I would talk to them all and let them know my thoughts about the roles and the direction of the city. During all of this, there were three ladies that really caught my interest. Though all three of them were very different, their commonality was that they were all tough-minded individuals and would make for stronger than expected opponents and great council members.

When the qualifying time for the city's elections came there were six people with their names in the hat, the three incumbents and the three ladies. As I watched the races unfold, it was clear the women were out working the men in these races. I would get calls about one of them knocking on a friend's door asking for their support or a photo of a newly planted sign in a yard. It became abundantly clear that these women really wanted to serve the people of their community and did not take anything for granted.

By the time election day rolled around I had concluded that the council for the city of Statesboro needed to go in a drastically different direction. I believed that the influence that one rogue council member had on the rest of the body was too great to risk the city's future on. Though I like each of the city councilmen as individuals, as a body I believed they were too weak to stand up to the bullying antics of the rogue member. Comparatively, I did believe that these ladies had the strength, will, and intelligence to help move this city in the direction that it needed to go.

When election day arrived, there was an energy in the city that said something big was about to happen. Prior to this day, I believed that there was going to be a new member on the city council and that was going to Paulette Chavers from district two. However, when it came to the other two races, I believed that they were going to be close and could go either way. What I also believed was that both Venus Mack and Shari Barr had put in the work to become the next council members for their districts.

I arrived at the election's office about an hour after the polls had closed. When I walked in, I saw the young volunteers from the campaigns sitting in the lobby waiting for the results to come in. Their nervous energy filled the room as we all made small talk in anticipation of the news. Then, emerging from her office, the election supervisor passed out the results. In a landslide victory Paulette Chavers defeated Sam Jones, Venus Mack, defeated Jeff Yawn by fourteen votes, and Shari Barr defeated Derek Duke by ten votes. And just like that, history was made. The City of Statesboro had elected not one but three women to serve on its council.

Since their election, I can't begin to imagine what it would have been like to navigate the perils of 2020 without them. I believe that many in this city do not recognize the jewels they have in these three remarkable human beings. They have been extremely hands-on as we have navigated the Covid crisis while rebuilding our city. Their hearts for the people of this city is evident in all they do.

Nearly four years later, our city and the world are in very different places than they were when I took my oath of office. When I was sworn into office, I understood that poverty was the greatest issue that was facing our city. It was my intent then, and still is today, to work to fix the systemic and institutional ills that perpetuates generational poverty. However, Covid-19 has increased the urgency of being able to address this matter and peeled away scabs of long festering wounds that our nation has yet to heal.

In February of 2020 the United States had its first known death to the coronavirus. For many Americans, the urgency to address the matter had not yet become a part of their reality and it was something that they heard about here and there on the news. However, the health professionals around the world were keeping a close eye on the deadly virus and were preparing for what many of them believed was the inevitable, the spread of the virus in the United States.

That same month my good friend Stephanie came to visit us. She had just returned from China the month before where she had been living for the past year or so. As I write this, I can still hear the urgency in her voice as she described to us what it was like living there as the virus was spreading throughout the country. She spoke of highway temperature checks and strict quarantines. As I listened, all these things were so alien at the time, but that would soon change.

Leaders and elected officials across the country began to get briefings from the Center for Disease Control, Department of Public Health and countless doctors and public health officials. In each of these briefings the message was the same. The threat is real. Lives are in danger and we must do everything we can to protect the people we serve.

If there was ever a time that Americans needed to put aside their political affiliations and do what was right for the nation, this was it. Unfortunately, that was not the case. Political expediency supplanted the need for open and honest dialog about a real threat to the American people. I can't think of any act that could have been more of a disservice to the American people. And as a result, as I write this epilogue, more than 530,000 Americans have lost their lives to the coronavirus. One hundred of those lives come from our small community.

While fighting off the coronavirus, America was slowed down just enough to shine a light on its age-old battle with racial disparities. As the coronavirus was beginning to spread in the United States, in Brunswick, GA Ahmaud Arbery was shot and killed while out jogging. In this disturbing video, Ahmaud was stalked and chased down by overzealous fools with guns. Even now, I fight back so many emotions as I think about the audacity of these men to take the life of another human being because they believed he was in the wrong neighborhood or resembled some phantom suspect. Then three short months later May 25, 2020 the world watched as officer Derek Chauvin kneeled on the neck of George Floyd for eight minutes and forty-six seconds. For many, this video showed the utter lack of humanity this officer had for George Floyd while for others it showed why we cry Black Lives Matter.

The summer of 2020, during a pandemic, was filled with marches for social justice across not just this nation, but around the world. And this was not missed by the people of the city of Statesboro. Hundreds of people of all colors and beliefs filled the courthouse square and marched in solidarity with the rest of the world. Our voices did not remain silent as we understood that our nation is strongest when we are together. In the largest election turnout in American history, those that took to the streets turned up at the polls that November.

The 2020 election showed both the power of the electorate and the fragility of the system. In an unprecedented grassroots campaign Joe Biden and those that supported him turned out more than eighty million people to the polls. And in doing so, they flipped the states of Georgia, Arizona, Pennsylvania, Wisconsin, and Michigan. Georgia, a state that had not gone Blue since 1992 with a Bill Clinton victory, repeated the feat in a Senatorial run-off election where Democrats John Ossoff and Raphael Warnock defeated incumbents David Purdue and Kelly Loeffler.

My journey to becoming mayor of my hometown has been an experience of a lifetime. Working to improve the quality of life for the people of the city while fighting off a global pandemic has pushed me to grow in ways that I had never imagined. However, the biggest lesson that I have learned is that there is no ego in service, especially when your mission is to always put the People Over Politics.

Now, on to the next run!